T0344463

Nonfunctional Requirements in Mobile Application Development

Nonfunctional Requirements in Mobile Application Development

Varun Gupta, Raj Kumar Chopra, and Durg Singh Chauhan

CRC Press
Taylor & Francis Group
Boca Raton London New York

CRC Press is an imprint of the
Taylor & Francis Group, an **informa** busines

First edition published 2021
by CRC Press
6000 Broken Sound Parkway NW, Suite 300, Boca Raton, FL 33487-2742
and by CRC Press
2 Park Square, Milton Park, Abingdon, Oxon, OX14 4RN

ISBN: 978-0-367-74071-9 (hbk)
ISBN: 978-0-367-75168-5 (pbk)
ISBN: 978-1-003-16092-2 (ebk)

Typeset in Adobe Garamond Pro
by KnowledgeWorks Global Ltd.

Contents

List of Tables and Figures

Tables

Figures

Editors

Varun Gupta received his PhD and Master of Technology (by research) in Computer Science and Engineering from the Uttarakhand Technical University and Bachelor of Technology (Hon's) from Himachal Pradesh University, respectively. He also holds an MBA (General) from Pondicherry University (A Central University).

Dr. Varun Gupta is working as a postdoctoral researcher with Universidade da Beira Interior, Portugal. He is also a visiting postdoctoral researcher, School of Business, FHNW University of Applied Sciences and Arts Northwestern Switzerland. He was an honorary research fellow of the University of Salford, Manchester, United Kingdom (2018–2021).

He is an associate editor for *IEEE Access* (Published by IEEE, SCIE Indexed with 4.098 impact factor), associate editor of *International Journal of Computer Aided Engineering and Technology* (Published by Inderscience Publishers, Scopus indexed), associate editor for IEEE Software Blog, associate editor of *Journal of Cases on Information Technology* (JCIT) (Published by IGI Global and Indexed by Emerging Sources Citation Index [ESCI] and SCOPUS) and former editorial team member of *British Journal of Educational Technology* (BJET) (Published by Wiley publishers, SCIE Indexed with 2.729 impact factor). He had been guest editor of many special issues published/ongoing with leading international journals and editor of many edited books to be published by IGI Global and Taylor & Francis Group (CRC Press).

He had organized many special sessions with Scopus indexed International Conferences worldwide, proceedings of which were published by Springer, IEEE and Elsevier. He is serving as a reviewer of IEEE Transactions on

Emerging Topics in Computational Intelligence. His area of interest is Evidence-based Software Engineering, Evolutionary Software Engineering (focusing on Requirements Management), Business Model Innovation and Innovation Management.

Raj Kumar Chopra received his PhD in the Business Management from GLA University and Bachelor of Technology in Electronics and Communication from Punjab Technical University. Dr. Raj Kumar Chopra is currently working in Bharat Sanchar Nigam Limited that is Govt. of India enterprise. He has an experience of 18 years in the field of mobile communication. He is associate editor of *Journal of Cases on Information Technology* (JCIT) (Published by IGI Global and Indexed by Emerging Sources Citation Index [ESCI] and SCOPUS). His area of interest is Mobile Communication, Networking and Value proposition innovation.

Prof. Durg Singh Chauhan is the pro-chancellor of GLA University, Mathura. He is the former vice-chancellor, Uttar Pradesh Technical University, Uttarakhand Technical University, Lovely Professional University, Jaypee University of Information Technology, GLA University and Secretary-General Association of Indian University (AIU). He has performed postdoctoral work at Goddard Space Flight Centre, Greenbelt Maryland, United States and is an alumnus of B.H.U., N.I.T. Tiruchirapalli and IIT Delhi. He began his illustrious career at Banaras Hindu University as a lecturer, reader and then professor.

Chapter 1

Introduction

1.1 General Introduction

The software industry aims to develop high-quality software for its clients under various development constraints. Huge expenditure is involved in an undertaking software project with failure risk threatening potential expected benefits. The m-commerce applications are very crucial for the business of product seller, and hence, any mistake done at part of the software developer takes seller business at stake. M-commerce apps are mobile apps, the success of which depends on both functional and nonfunctional requirements (NFRs). These m-commerce apps must be developed using matured and dynamic software development methodologies. The requirements of such mobile m-commerce apps are highly sophisticated as compared to desktop or web applications. The research work will analyze the status of mobile software development from implementation of NFR for generic mobile apps. The results will be equally valid for m-commerce apps.

The ability of the software to satisfy its customer results in enhanced customer base, implying higher software sales and huge turnover. The reverse of this situation negates the justification of investment of huge development costs. The failure not only creates a monetary loss in the current project but may also impact the company reputation, thereby decreasing the customer base of new projects to be undertaken by the firm. Customer satisfaction is a prime business value for the firm and the company's future depends on it.

Satisfaction comes from the ability of the software to meet the expectation of its customers/users. These customers are mainly concerned with the functionality of the software, i.e. functional requirements of the software, and hence, nonfunctional ones are unseen initially.

However, if the same NFR remains unimplemented, functional requirement may become obsolete as they may be unable to deliver without nonfunctional areas or may be unusable till nonfunctional ones are implemented. Thus, the neglect of nonfunctional ones may lead to complete the rejection of the software amongst the stakeholders/customers, even though they never requested them.

In case of mobile software development, various challenges get mapped to various NFRs like GUI, interactions with a large number of other apps, location aware services, security hardware and software independence apart from other traditional challenges like usability, performance and reliability. Software developers must consider these different issues in the form of NFRs during the development of the mobile apps. These issues can never be predefined and in fact depend on the level of expertise of the software developer.

For example, a software developer must consider the issue of database consistency as mobile networks usually perform handoffs. In case of availability of a high-speed network, it is possible to increase the data transfer speed during transaction execution, thereby making the consistency issues as one of the important NFRs. The successful implementation of the mobile app depends on the ability of the software developer to implement not only functional but also NFRs by anticipating future events led by technological changes, environmental changes etc.

Numerous techniques are available to elicit software requirements and to prioritize these requirements. The available techniques focus mainly on functional requirements that are available in the literature, and very little work is available that handles NFRs separately or at least relative to functional requirements.

Keeping in view the importance of NFR in successful implementation of projects, especially mobile apps, the need is felt to undertake a survey of existing mobile apps developments from the viewpoint of NFR contributions.

Effort is ongoing in the direction to analyze the contribution of NFRs to success/failure rates of the product, analyze the status of NFRs, and its implementation and contributions to the cost and time of overall development. Efforts are made to analyze the variation with increase in the size of organization and complexity of the projects.

Further, there is a need to study the impact of missing NFRs on the business success rates of both the software developing firms and the client firms who employs the system for delivering their produced goods and services in economy. Thus, the impact analysis is performed employing the survey of many firms at two independent levels—*developing firm level* and *client firm level*. The former deals with the impact analysis of missing NFRs from the developed software on software firm business while later deals with the impact analysis of missing NFRs from the purchased software by the firm on its goods/services business. There is a need to undertake an empirical study to investigate that how much and in what direction there is an impact of missing NFRs and the business success.

NFRs must be selected for implementation together with functional requirements to enhance the success of software projects. Three approaches exist for performing the prioritization of NFRs using the suitable prioritization technique. There is a need to analyze the accuracy of individual approaches and the variation of accuracy with the complexity of the software project. The objective is to see if individual prioritization of NFRs is better or the prioritization with functional one. The new prioritization techniques for NFRs in accordance with the outcome of the experiment are kept as future work.

The complete research will include various empirical methods like literature survey, industrial project survey, academic project survey and case studies, wherever applicable. The case study will be undertaken in the form of analysis of historical documents and personal observation to verify, validate and/or add more to the analysis information of the industrial and academic project survey. The advantage is that the researchers will get the opportunity to see if the practice adopted by survey participants is industry specific or generally followed across many firms.

Further, the wrong or misleading information due to different terminologies in literature and industries will be minimized as a result of observations through the case studies. Case studies undertaken by the researchers given them the opportunity to verify the insight brought up by the survey participants with the things observed by the researchers. The collected data will be subjected for necessary analysis individually and against each other.

1.2 Terminology

1.2.1 Requirement Prioritization

The software projects are getting more complex day by day due to an increased number of users and ever-changing needs. Further, there is a reduction in time to market and enhanced need for high quality due to ever growing competition. Every requirement is bearing a cost and time to implement which makes the idea of implementing all requirements in "one go" completely bad idea. Under such circumstances, the software engineer adopts techniques called requirement prioritization to select the high priority requirements. This allows the organization to release multiple versions of the same software.

Requirement prioritization is an activity to perform the selection of requirements, the task that is challenging due to the involvement of many stakeholders with potentially conflicting view points, multiple requirements to be handled and large effort to be invested in this activity. The wrong requirement selection not only results in wasteful effort and potentially increased effort of the next release, but also possesses the risk of project failures. There are different techniques for undertaking the software prioritization that varies in terms of computational algorithms, complexities, measurement scale etc.

1.2.2 Nonfunctional Requirements

The NFRs are the requirements that defines that how the functional requirements will be implemented. In other words, NFRs place constraints on the implementation on functional requirements. Such requirements do not provide any functionality to end user but are required for efficient implementation of functional requirements or proper working of the software.

It had been widely accepted that customers do not want NFRs since they do not offer any functionality; however, customer may refuse to use the software due to missing NFRs. The reason is functionality will be effectively implemented only if few NFRs and constraints are also implemented by the developer. Such requirements are not elicited from users but are implemented by developer, and it is difficult to convince the user/customer about NFRs.

NFRs require special focus during requirement engineering activity because the ignoring few NFR may lead to complete failure of the mobile applications. This is because the user expectations from the experience from executing the app on the mobile phone are different compared to the desktop computing machines. The mobile devices impose server restrictions on the development of the mobile apps because of the restrictions imposed by their working environments including limited resolution, working conditions of the mobile components, bandwidth limitations, storage limitations and energy utilization issues. This imposes conditions on the development of the mobile apps in order to execute them with high performance in tightly constrained mobile infrastructure.

1.2.3 Empirical Studies

According to Wikipedia, the empirical research is defined as "a way of gaining knowledge by means of direct and indirect observation or experience". In other words, empirical research involves the collection of primary data by the means of either direct observation and/or experience of the field under investigation and the analysis of the collected data to draw meaningful conclusions. Empirical research helps researchers to undergo through various types of studies like exploratory, descriptive, explanatory and experimental research. Different types of research are carried out with different objectives using different tools. For example, exploratory study is carried out to explore new field using surveys of literature etc., while descriptive one involves getting descriptions of the elements of interest to researchers using interviews, case studies, etc. Researcher can do empirical research by using different methods like case studies, surveys and experiments. The surveys are conducted when the samples are too many and lot of broad information is to be collected, and case studies are conducted to gain deeper insights about elements of interests and experiments could be conducted to investigate the impact of one variable over another which could be conducted in controlled and uncontrolled manner.

1.3 Aim and Objective of Book

The aim of the book is to study the importance and the impact of NFRs on overall software project. This includes studying impact on metrics like project success or failure rates, development cost and time. The book also aims to analyze the current status of NFRs during development of mobile applications and suggests optimal ways of integrating the NFR during requirement selection activity.

The aim is fulfilled by attaining the following objectives:

1. To study the impact of NFRs on mobile application development in both industry and academics.

    This objective is achieved by carrying out empirical study employing case studies and surveys of industrial and academic mobile application projects. The individual empirical results are analyzed with the results of systematic literature survey.

2. To analyze the accuracy of NFR prioritization approaches for different complexity projects—this analysis is useful in attainment of the following objective:

This objective is that achieved NFRs must be selected for implementation together with functional requirements to enhance the success of software projects. Three approaches exist for performing the prioritization of NFRs using the suitable prioritization technique. This objective is achieved by performing experimentation on three different complexity versions of the industrial software project using a cost-value prioritization technique employing three approaches. Experimentation is conducted to analyze the accuracy of individual approaches and the variation of accuracy with the complexity of the software project.

3. To study the impact of NFRs on m- commerce business success.

This objective is achieved by carrying out interview-based survey of business organization that is able to make their business offering available to its buyers through an m-commerce application. The organizations have given quantitative data as answer to the question that aims to analyze the impact of NFRs on business success. The collected data are then subjected to testing of a formulated hypothesis using statistical testing approaches.

1.4 Problem Statement

This book tries to find a solution to the problems stated as follows: "What is the status of mobile application development in the software industry from the viewpoint of NFRs for different complexity projects developed using different development strategies by matured and less matured organizations?". Further the book tries to identify the impact of the NFRs on business success and failure of both the software developing firm and clients firms offering goods and services through purchased software in economy.

1.5 Research Framework

The three objectives of the research were briefly outlined in Section 1.5 of the chapter. The fulfillment of the objectives makes it possible to find through an empirical study on the state of affairs of handling of NFRs by the software developing firms involved in delivery of mobile apps like m-commerce apps. This involves the investigation of not only the practices, procedures and methods of handling NFRs but also to analyze the contribution of NFRs in project parameters like product success rates, failure rates, overall cost and time for different organizations and project sizes.

This further requires the work to investigate the impact of NFRs on business success and failure of not only the firms procuring the software for delivery of goods/services but also the firm involved in the software development.

The overall outcome of this book will be a motivation for both the software developing firms to focus on NFRs and also to firms procuring the developed software to invest resources that attract software developers to handle NFRs.

The research framework established by the book is given in Figure 1.1.

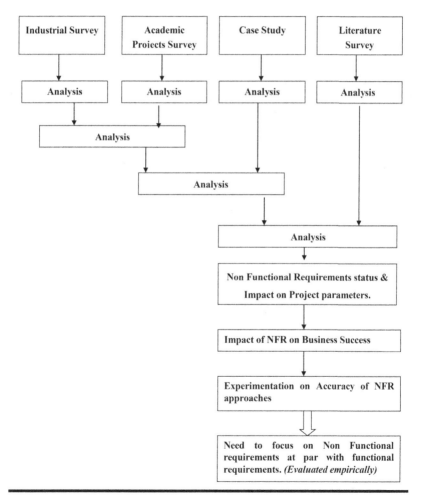

Figure 1.1   Research framework.

1.6 Outline of Book

This book is organized into six chapters. Each chapter is based on different research objectives and research methodology. The outcome from each chapter helps to find solutions to the problem as framed in Section 1.6 of this chapter. The details of different chapters are as followings:

Chapter 1: Introduction

This chapter introduces the audience to the research context, basics of the terms used in book, problem statement and research methodology used in the book. The various established objectives, outcomes and organization of the book are given in this chapter.

Chapter 2: Literature Survey

This chapter positions the work given in this book with respect to the resources available in the literature. The contribution of NFRs to project success and various prioritization practices are the outlines in this chapter. The systematic literature survey is carried out on few bibliographic databases and outcome is reported thereafter.

Chapter 3: Impact of NFR on Business Success

This chapter tries to study the impact of a number of missing NFRs on the business success rates of both the software developing firms and the client firms that employ the system for delivering their produced goods and services in economy. The samples of 135 representatives from developing firms and 170 from clients participated in survey through questionnaire and interview sessions. The sampled data were subjected to chi-square testing, and the results proved that the number of missing NFRs impacts the business success of the firms. The larger the missing NFRs—the larger the impact on business success, and the firm moves toward failures.

Chapter 4: Status of Nonfunctional Requirement in Mobile Application Development: An Empirical Study

This chapter undertakes an empirical study available for analyzing the contribution of NFRs. In order to suggest mechanisms for improving product success rates, it is important to undertake the empirical study through surveys and case studies in industrial and academic mobile app projects to analyze the software development practices focused on NFRs. The analysis of data collected through empirical methods suggests that NFRs are handled in the rough ad hoc fashion and the number is very little relative to functional requirements. The contribution to cost and time is smaller due to a smaller number of requirements and will increase considerably with the increase in NFRs. The impact of NFRs on product success rates, failure rates, overall cost and time varies with type of development, size of organization and complexity of the undertaken mobile app projects.

Chapter 5: Status of Nonfunctional Requirement in Mobile Application Development in Academic Projects

This chapter undertakes an empirical study on academic projects. The ups and downs learned during academic projects help students to update their project database that could provide learning experience with industrial projects. The academic projects could find their applicability in industries, and hence, the quality of such software is important. Quality depends on the quality of software engineering practices. It is thus important to analyze that state of software development from NFRs point of view. The study is based on the objectives as established for industrial and literature studies performed in Chapters 2 and 3 of this book. This work is an extension of the work given in previous chapters but in academic environment settings.

To answer the seven research questions as framed in Chapters 2 and 3 of this book, 30 final-year and passed-out students belonging to both B. Tech and M. Tech academic programs were interviewed to get answers of the research questions.

Chapter 6: Accuracy of Nonfunctional Requirement Prioritization Approaches for Different Complexity Projects: An Experimentation

This chapter of the book performs experimentation on three different complexity versions of the industrial software project using cost-value prioritization technique employing three approaches. Experimentation is conducted to analyze the accuracy of individual approaches of NFR prioritization and the variation of accuracy with the complexity of the software project. The results indicate that selecting NFRs separately but in accordance with functionality has higher accuracy amongst the other two approaches. Further, likewise other approaches, it witnesses the decrease in accuracy with increase in software complexity but the decrease is minimal.

Chapter 7: Conclusion and Future Work

This chapter concludes that the NFRs are equally important like functional requirements. Likewise a functional requirement that ensures utility of the software, NFRs ensures the effective implementation of functionality. Such requirements impact the project success by impacting parameters like quality, cost, time and impact the business success of developing firms and client firms. The impact of missing NFRs is too hard for the business and such business may be out of the market depending on severity, number and criticality of the NFRs.

In future, it is expected that a suitable requirement prioritization techniques will be proposed that strikes a balance between functional and NFRs. It is expected that the outcome of this book will motivate both the researchers and firms to invest resources to handle NFRs. It is expected that in the near future, NFRs–based prioritization techniques will be evaluated on both project and business success parameters to evaluate the success.

1.7 Scope of Book

This book performs an empirical study of NFRs, which includes the analysis of their contribution, practices, impact on project and business models. The study is done by considering the mobile apps as they, like m-commerce apps, are having a large number of functional requirements, and current businesses have migrated to various mobile apps including m-commerce apps. Keeping in view the easy availability of samples and dynamic nature of mobile apps, the study is performed in mobile domains.

The research in proposing a new prioritization method for NFRs is out of the scope of this book. The book just investigates the NFRs' contributions and provides enough motivations to the business and research community.

1.8 Summary

This chapter of the book sets the basic research context that is being investigated and presented throughout the remaining chapters of the book.

Chapter 2

Literature Review

2.1 Review of the Status of Nonfunctional Requirement in Mobile Application Development[*]

To achieve the aim and objectives as stated in Chapter 1, the empirical study was conducted to analyze the status of nonfunctional requirements (NFRs) during the development of mobile applications. The study was conducted through empirical methods like case studies and surveys (Chapter 3) and literature surveys to analyze the NFR status and explore their relationship with project metrics. The study also explores the manner in which NFRs are handled during the release planning activity. An attempt is made to study how the collected answers vary with the project complexity, maturity and size of the software organization.

In order to conduct the empirical study systematically and exhaustively, the systematic literature was reviewed against predefined bibliographic databases, selecting the research papers that satisfied the criteria as laid down in Table 2.1. The extracted papers must be able to answer the framed research questions (Section 3.4).

---

[*] This article titled "**Status of Nonfunctional Requirements in Mobile Application Development: An Empirical Study**", appears in **Journal of Information Technology Research (JITR) (ISSN 1938-7857; eISSN 1938-7865),** Vol 10, Issue 1, **Copyright 2017, IGI Global,** www.igi-global.com. **Reprinted by permission of the publisher.**

Table 2.1   Inclusion and Exclusion Criteria

Inclusion Criteria	Exclusion Criteria
1. The papers having the potential of answering at least one research question. 2. Papers containing information related to nonfunctional requirements, mobile app process models, individual development activities and development metric values like cost, time and success and failure rates of only mobile applications. 3. Papers addressing any research type like exploratory, explanatory, descriptive and experimental, covering information as given in point 2.	1. Papers not yielding answers to any research question. 2. Papers not related to mobile applications.

The objective is to analyze the available research work reported by the researchers in the form of research solutions, case studies, surveys, experimental work to establish state of being, report phenomena involved, report constituent activities or to compare existing works.

The literature is surveyed in the form of systematic literature surveys (SLRs) following the guidelines available in Kitchenham and Charters (2007). The guidelines of SLR suggest the undertaking of the activities contained in three phases such as planning the review, conducting the review and reporting the review. The SLR involves searching suitable resources like journals, conferences and workshop research materials in accordance with the review protocol defined during the planning phase. The extracted data are subjected to analysis/synthesis and the SLR is reported in the form of a report.

The SLR is based on the objective of getting the answers to the six research questions framed in this book based on the data available in the literature. The required information may be available as a full research paper or may exist as a section or subsection. The search string must be able to extract those papers also that have minute information capable of answering the framed questions. The search/query string is framed as "Non-Functional Requirements AND Mobile Applications". The string is expected to trigger databases for all the papers that have the information of NFRs related to mobile applications. The papers disseminating the prioritization techniques, process model, various development metric values, evaluations and empirical results are likely to be extracted if available. This limits the scope of a survey of the available work connecting software engineering activities with NFRs.

The papers matching the keywords of query string are put to selection to extract meaningful papers in accordance with the inclusion and exclusion criteria defined in Table 2.1.

The below-mentioned databases are triggered against the formulated query string:

- IEEE Xplore
- ScienceDirect
- ACM Digital Library
- SpringerLink
- Taylor & Francis.

The triggering of the database was subjected to the mentioned search parameters apart from consideration of inclusion and exclusion criteria (Table 2.1).

- Research papers must be published in bibliographic databases from 2012 to 2015.
- The research journals, transactions and conference publications are only considered.
- The journals and conferences must be related to computer science and/or project management. This also includes the journals involving decision systems, mobile systems and empirical studies related to computers/management.

The triggering of the abovementioned databases yielded many papers that are subjected to multiple layers of selections using title, abstract, content and references, as depicted in Figure 2.1.

A total of 691 papers were subjected to a rigorous selection in accordance with inclusion and exclusion criteria by reading the title, abstract and body text. The references were analyzed to see if any of the reference list papers could be added in accordance with the ability to answer any research question and whether it satisfied the inclusion and exclusion criteria. None of the papers was selected from the reference list. Finally, the list was analyzed to see if the same paper appeared multiple times. In total, six papers were selected.

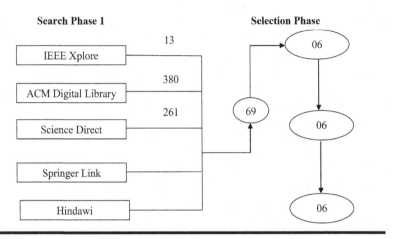

Figure 2.1   Literature survey.

The research works available in the literature as extracted through the SLR are limited in scope and nature. Hence, their capability to answer all the questions is very limited. The data required for answering a few questions like those based on cost, time, success rates, failure rates are not reported in qualitative or quantitative terms in the extracted papers. Minute chunks of information given in the extracted papers were glued together to "best possible guess" answer to the framed questions. The extracted papers are presented in the research question sections to which they better provide a complete or partial answer.

RQ 1. What is the extent to which nonfunctional requirements get the software developers' attraction?

The special issue editorial in Capilla et al. (2012) reported that applications like mobile applications, complex web-based systems, self-adaptive software and real-time systems demand for high-quality software to work. High quality means implementation of NFRs that include requirements like reliability, modifiability, performance and usability (Chung et al., 2009; Laplante et al., 2009; Capilla et al., 2012). The special issue editorial does not specify any method specific to handling of NFRs of mobile applications.

Hindle (2015) reports the methodology that software developers of mobile applications (smartphone or tablet) can employ to investigate if the new change request has potential threat of increasing battery consumption. Other NFRs are out of the scope of the abovementioned paper.

Fernandes et al. (2014) emphasize the need for evaluation of the performance of mobile application to provide the best experience to the users. Good experience represents the high level of customer satisfaction and depends on high performance of the application. The performance includes execution time of application, response time of application and an efficient use of system hardware. The author replied on the findings of the two case studies as experimental subjects, and it was reported that the evaluation results can be used by developers to make design decision during software development.

Orsini et al. (2015) classified the mobile cloud computing applications into availability, portability, scalability, usability, maintainability and security (considering the ISO criteria for software quality as baseline). The guidelines are also provided to developers for designing mobile cloud computing (MCC) mobile applications.

The literature lacks the research information that highlights the manner the mobile app developers select the NFRs for implementation. Further, there is no agreement among the researchers about particular NFRs to be implemented. The work reports the importance of implementation of NFRs only.

RQ 2. What is the cost and time percentage of NFR in the overall project cost and duration?

The extracted paper does not specify the cost and time percentage of NFRs to the total cost and development time. However, the NFRs are costlier and time-consuming to be implemented. An educated guess could be made about the cost and time by analyzing the data given in Table 2.2 and those reported in Svensson et al. (2013) about a number of functional requirements (FRs) and NFRs. The number of NFRs is less for small- or medium-complexity projects and little larger for incrementally developed mobile apps by large organizations. Large organizations will have reusable code and experiences, so the overall implementation cost and time of NFRs would be smaller but larger than those developed by small or medium organizations (due to a little larger number of NFRs).

RQ 3. What is the implementation status of NFR to FR for different complexity projects?

Norbert Seyff et al. (2015) carried out a study to evaluate the impact of social networking sites like Facebook on increasing the participation of geographically distributed users of the software in three main activities

Table 2.2 Requirement Details for Different Mobile Apps of Each Case Study (Norbert Seyff et al., 2015)

Sl. No.	Case Study	No. of Groups	Group Number	No. of stakeholders (contributing people)	Functional Requirements (FRs)	Nonfunctional Requirements (NFRs)	Ratio of NFR to FR
1.	I	8	Gr 1	12	82	18	0.22
			Gr 2	4	90	10	0.11
			Gr 3	11	73	27	0.37
			Gr 4	4	75	25	0.33
			Gr 5	7	90	10	0.11
			Gr 6	5	69	31	0.45
			Gr 7	6	83	17	0.20
			Gr 8	8	100	0	0.00
2.	II	6	Sof 1	6	46	54	1.17
			Sof 2	5	29	71	2.45
			Sof 3	5	36	64	1.78
			Fof 1	7	74	26	0.35
			Fof 2	2	79	21	0.27
			Fof 3	3	80	20	0.25

3.	III	9					
			Gr 1	10	79	21	0.27
			Gr 2	5	63	38	0.60
			Gr 3	4	50	50	1.00
			Gr 4	7	73	27	0.37
			Gr 5	11	77	23	0.30
			Gr 6	7	86	14	0.16
			Gr 7	7	72	28	0.39
			Gr 8	2	92	8	0.09
			Gr 9	6	87	13	0.15

Note: Authors had identified many duplicate requirements among FRs and NFRs (columns 6 and 7 of Table 2.2). The requirements excluding duplicates were termed as distinct requirements.

of requirement engineering like elicitation, prioritization and negotiation. The authors carried out the impact analysis using three exploratory case studies. Each case study involved a different number of users and students. A different number of Facebook groups were formed for each case study, with each group performing requirement engineering activity on different mobile apps. The number of stakeholders (students and users), the number of groups and the number of FRs and NFRs per case study are given in Table 2.2.

Svensson et al. (2013) reported the number of quality requirements (NFRs) by analyzing requirement specifications belonging to different subdomains. The reported data represents the small number of NFRs to the number of FRs. A total of 294 quality requirements exhibit both functional and quality aspects, 1351 are FRs and 533 purely quality requirements. Quality requirements are calculated to be 827. The ratio is very small for few domains and somewhat higher for other domains (minimum 13% and maximum 92%). However, for all the subdomains taken together, there are 827 NFRs (including 294 nonfunctional ones with functional aspects) against 2178 total requirements or 38% nonfunctional ones. The ratio comes out to be 0.38 (827/2178) or 0.40 (533/3178).

Comparing the results with the results in Chapter 4, Table 4.7, the ratio is smaller in the latter case. The surveyed projects in the former case are developed incrementally by large organization, while projects shown in Table 2.2 are small-/medium-complexity projects (non-incremental). Ratios are higher for incremental projects developed by the large organization.

RQ 4. What are the typical categories of NFRs implemented by mobile software developers?

The various NFRs identified for a few mobile apps are given in Table 2.3. The identified NFRs are not exhaustive but only those suitable for undertaking the research study.

RQ 5. How are Nonfunctional Requirements prioritized?

There are plenty of papers that suggest different ways of prioritizing the software requirements. The largest numbers of techniques are available for prioritization of FRs. However, the research aiming for prioritization of NFRs alone or at least together with functional ones is limited. Few prioritization

Table 2.3 Identified Nonfunctional Requirement

Sl. No.	Paper Reference	Nonfunctional Requirements
1.	Chung et al. (2009), Laplante et al. (2009); Capilla et al. (2012)	Reliability, modifiability, performance and usability.
2.	Hindle (2015)	Battery consumption.
3.	Fernandes et al. (2014)	Performance, efficient use of system hardware.
4.	Orsini et al. (2015)	Availability, portability, scalability, usability, maintainability and security.
5.	Norbert Seyff et al. (2015)	(Case study I): look and feel, usability requirements, performance, environmental, security and cultural requirements (4.3%). (Case study II): look and feel, usability, performance and environmental issues. (Case study III): usability, look and feel, performance, operation and environment, security and legal.

techniques are suggested in generic form, meaning it's not specific if requirements mean either functional or nonfunctional or both. In many such research papers, the proposal is evaluated on the software with many FRs. Hence, the challenges that may occur when NFRs are prioritized together with functional ones remain untested and generated impacts remained untested. Limited work is available that aims to evaluate different prioritization techniques considering both FRs and NFRs. One such study is carried out in Dabbagh et al. (2015), but the reported controlled experiment is carried out on 20 requirements of automated teller machine (ATM), cash deposit machine (CDM) and check deposit machine (CQM) that is not a mobile application. The challenge would have been employing the innovative and challenging NFRs of mobile applications that are not there in desktop or web applications.

The available prioritization techniques do not specify if they are applicable for mobile apps or not. The software selected for validation of the proposal is mostly desktop-based or web-based application.

The SLR did not extract any of the papers based on the prioritization or evaluation of prioritization techniques of generic software product requirements (generic means mobile applications and NFRs not specified). The scope of the survey was confined to the study of NFRs of mobile applications only. However, the authors in Norbert Seyff et al. (2015) employed a generic requirement engineering model with the usual activities of elicitation, prioritization and negotiation. The model employs the social networking site, Facebook, for having user participation. The model is employed by students and invited Facebook friends in all three case studies to carry out requirement engineering activities on mobile application domains. The applicability of the proposal in real app development is unsure.

RQ 6. What is the extent to which the answers to the above questions depend on the maturity and size of software organization?

The limited work was available in the literature that focused on mobile application development from NFRs point of view. The extracted papers are not able to answer many research questions and the limited available work does not specify the information that allows inference about the impact of maturity and size of organization together with the nature of development on variations of collected information that is organized under suitable answers to the framed research question. Analyzing the number of requirements reported for a few projects by other researchers, maturity of organizations has an impact on the number of NFRs in projects. The ratio is higher for incremental projects implemented by large organizations. It is smaller for typically one-go projects implemented by small or medium organizations. However, the variation of the number of such requirements with the change in complexity of the project is an unknown phenomenon due to lack of information available in the literature.

RQ 7. How the present practices of the mobile development firms impact project success and failure rates?

Unfortunately, the researchers were not able to gather evidence of impact of missing NFR on product success. It does not mean that there is no impact, but it means that it was not reported in the extracted papers.

2.2 Review of Requirement Prioritization Approaches for Nonfunctional Requirement

Numerous requirement prioritization techniques have been proposed in literature. The techniques differ in computational algorithm, measurement scale and efficiency in handling requirements. The requirement prioritization techniques include the EasyWinWin methodology (Gruenbacher, 2000), financially informed requirement prioritization (Huang and Denne, 2005), the cost-value approach (Karlsson and Ryan, 1997), value-oriented prioritization (VOP) (Jim et al., 2007), Weiger's method (Weiger, 1999a, 1999b), the hybrid assessment method (Ribeiro et al., 2011), different requirement prioritization techniques (Gupta and Srivastav, 2011; Gupta et al., 2012a, 2013a, 2015a, 2015b, 2016) and many more. These are generic techniques and do not specify how NFRs are to be prioritized. However, limited techniques for prioritization of NFRs are available in Daneva et al. (2007), Dabbagh and Lee (2014), Mylopoulos et al. (1992), Dabbagh and Lee (2014), etc. Limited work is available related to analysis of NFRs in industries as in Svensson et al. (2011) and Doerr et al. (2015).

Pairwise-based requirement prioritization techniques are found to be more accurate than non-pairwise-based prioritizations (Karlsson, 1996; Karlsson et al., 1998; Perini et al., 2009). Pairwise comparisons do increase the number of comparisons as requirements increase leading to scalability problem (Karlsson et al., 1998; Karlsson et al., 2004; Ahl, 2005; Perini et al., 2009; Ribeiro et al., 2011; Voola and Babu, 2013; Achimugu et al., 2014). Further, different researchers had compared different prioritization techniques in different environments and using different data sets as in Karlsson (1996), Karlsson et al. (1998), Karlsson et al. (2004), Berander (2004), Avesani et al. (2005), Lehtola et al. (2004), Lehtola et al. (2006), Perini et al. (2007), etc. However, there is lack of a generalized theory among the researchers about the applicability of different techniques given the different inputs and environments.

Further, requirement prioritization had found its utility in different activities like decision aspect prioritization and regression testing as available in Gupta et al. (2011b, 2012a, 2012b, 2013a), Srikanth and Williams (2005), Srikanth et al. (2005) and Srivastav et al. (2008). Reprioritization is growing to be another area that is putting much pressure on requirement prioritization practices. Reprioritization practices are proposed in Gupta et al. (2015c), Racheva et al. (2008), Bakalova et al. (2011), Racheva et al., 2010a, 2010b, Kukreja and Boehm (2012) and Gupta et al. (2013a).

There is a lack of NFR prioritization approaches and empirical studies of the importance of the NFRs.

Chapter 3

Impact of NFR's on M-Commerce Business Success

3.1 Introduction

The software industries are involved in the development of software for clients. The clients need the software to run their business. For example, a leather company may require a mobile app for selling their products online. Such an app is developed by a software firm, the charges of which are normally recovered through per unit sale of the product through the developed m-commerce app. Doerr et al. (2005) has reported that the nonfunctional requirements (NFRs) of the product determine the business success as it differentiates the firm from its competitors. The NFRs are the requirements that define that how the functional requirements will be implemented. In other words, NFRs place constraints on the implementation on functional requirements. Such requirements do not provide any functionality to end user but are required for efficient implementation of functional requirements or proper working of the software.

The missing NFRs from the developed software will impact business of both the developing firm and client firm. Thus, the impact analysis is performed employing the survey of many firms at two independent levels—the *developing firm level* and the *client firm level*. The former deals with the impact analysis of missing NFRs from the developed software on the software firm business while the later deals with the impact analysis of missing NFRs from the purchased software by the firm on its goods/services business.

Techniques for prioritization of NFRs do exist in the literature as proposed in Daneva et al. (2007), Dabbagh and Lee (2014), Mylopoulos et al. (1992), Dabbagh and Lee (2014) etc. Limited work is also available related to an analysis of NFRs in industries as in Svensson et al. (2011), Doerr et al. (2005). The impact of NFRs on different project parameters like product success rates, failure rates, overall cost and time for different organizations and project sizes was studied through an empirical study (Gupta et al., 2016). The impact was reported to be positive. However, the project success is different from process success and business success. Project and process success may or may not hit business success depending on the criticality of NFRs. However, to the best of author's knowledge, the empirical work aiming to study the impact of missing NFRs of the software product on business success is missing from the literature.

Thus, the impact analysis aims to study the impact of missing NFRs on business that in the first case is on developing firm itself, while in another, it is upon the firm purchasing the software.

The outcome of this paper will motivate both the developing firm and the client firm about the importance of NFRs.

3.2 Data Collection

The impact analysis is to be performed on two different independent levels with different objectives and different business success parameters. Thus, the data are collected through the questionnaires followed by interviews of the representatives of the software developing firms and clients firms that have entered price agreements with the developing firms. There is no one to one relation between the studied cases of developing and client firms because it was difficult to identify the representatives of the client firm say X that has purchased low quality software from firm say Y. The firms that have agreed to provide data are those that have agreed to the realities of success and failures of the businesses in terms of the following metrics:

Success metrics for developing firms

- **Satisfaction of client firm:** The change requests are usual thing in software development. However, in case some NFRs are missing, which is going to hit business hard for clients, then a situation may emerge where clients get aggressive behavior and pressures for quick and fix–type implementations. Satisfied clients usually have normal behavior and gives times for changes.
- **Developing of networks:** After the delivery of the product, the firms usually try to take an advantage of the built-in relations by either trying to enter into new product agreements or influencing the "friend" companies of the client. So two metrics were of prime interests, i.e. new agreements and friend agreements.
- **Revenues:** Firms charges for additional functionality. If the client is satisfied then he may be happy paying for the extra features.

Success metrics for client firms

- **Satisfaction of customer:** The marketing department usually does customer surveys that why the customers are or are not using the developed software in comparison to usage scenarios with competitor's similar product. Product developed may be fine or service offered may be good, but the delivery software (purchased one) may not be able to retain the customers. The data relevant to the dissatisfied customers due to missing NFRs are of prime interest.
- **Revenues:** Firms usually give good discounts or reward for purchasing done through apps like m-commerce apps. Large sales mean large revenues, which reflect that the customers are happy with the app.

The data were collected using the scale of low, medium and high. The firm representatives had experience of many projects. Some had experience where product has many missing NFRs while some had experience with products with large missing NFRs. Thus, for each project, success metrics were given values using the scale mentioned earlier. The NFRs were also divided into three categories—low, medium and high representing the number of NFRs missing from the released software. Thus, if the less number of NFRs are missing (represented by "low") and impact is medium then the value stores under row labeled with "low" and column labeled with "medium" gets increments by one. Thus, each cell contains the value that is aggregation of total number of projects impacted with respect to missing requirements.

The total 135 representatives from developing firm and 170 from client firm participated. The firms are small, medium and large organizations including starts-ups. The interviews were held with the representatives to explore the relation between NFRs and business success.

3.3 Hypothesis Formulation

Separate hypotheses set, i.e. null and alternate hypotheses, are created for both developing and clients firms. These are given as follows:

For developing firm

Ho$_1$: There is no relation between the NFRs and the business success.
Ha$_1$: There is a relation between the NFRs and the business success.

For developing firm

Ho$_2$: There is no relation between the NFRs and the business success.
Ha$_2$: There is a relation between the NFRs and the business success.

3.4 Results

The collected data were subjected to statistical analysis using the open-source software online statistical tool for chi-square testing as available online at http://www.socscistatistics.com/tests/chisquare2/Default2.aspx. The collected data were analyzed for checking the relation between the missing number of requirements and business success. The collected data are shown in Tables 3.1, 3.2, 3.3 and 3.4 for both developing and client firms.

3.5 Hypothesis Testing

The collected data (Tables 3.1–3.5) are subjected to chi-square testing to test the framed hypothesis. The statistical software for chi-square testing as available online at http://www.socscistatistics.com/tests/chisquare2/Default2.aspx is used to perform chi-square testing. This testing is employed because the variable under test is categorical variables. Each table will be subjected for

Table 3.1 Developing Firm Data About Client Firm Satisfaction

Sl. No.	Missing NFR	Number in Sample*	Satisfaction of Client Firm		
			Low	Medium	High
1.	Low	100	5	45	50
2.	Med	50	40	6	4
3.	High	40	39	1	0

*Representatives had different experiences with products with different missing requirements.

Table 3.2 Developing Firm Data About Developing of Networks

Sl. No.	Missing NFR	Number in Sample	Developing of Networks		
			Low	Medium	High
1.	Low	100	5	70	25
2.	Med	50	46	4	0
3.	High	40	40	0	0

Table 3.3 Developing Firm Data About Revenues

Sl. No.	Missing NFR	Number in Sample	Revenues		
			Low	Medium	High
1.	Low	100	5	45	50
2.	Med	50	40	6	4
3.	High	40	39	1	0

Table 3.4 Client Firm Data About Customer Satisfaction

Sl. No.	Missing NFR	Number in Sample	Customer Satisfaction		
			Low	Medium	High
1.	Low	120	7	49	63
2.	Med	40	38	2	0
3.	High	10	40	0	0

Table 3.5   Client Firm Data About Revenues

Sl. No.	Missing NFR	Number in Sample	Revenues		
			Low	Medium	High
1.	Low	120	7	49	63
2.	Med	40	38	2	0
3.	High	10	40	0	0

the chi-square test. The result of running the online chi square tool on data collected from samples is given in Table 3.6.

Running the chi-square test using online chi-square tool gives the following values of chi-square at alpha level of confidence of 0.05, i.e. $\alpha = 0.05$.

3.6 Result Analysis

The data collected represent the experience of the firms with missing NFRs. The chi-square test revealed that the missing NFRs impact the business of both developing firms and client firms. The degree of impact will depend on the number and criticality of missing NFRs.

However, variation in the frequency values of the cells of Tables 3.1–3.5 made the authors excited to hear from the representatives about few interesting points given as follows:

- Representatives told the authors that missing NFRs has a direct impact on customer satisfaction and developing of networks (inverse relationship). However, the data values do not matches for Tables 3.1 and 3.2. For this, representatives told us that no doubt the development of relations depends heavily on quality of product delivered in the market, but even if you deliver something great, the greatness will not be proportional to network building. Other factors like brand image and competitor play an important role. Of course, the revenues depend on customer satisfaction.
- Increase in number of missing NFRs makes it difficult to retain the customer on the app when almost every competitor has app- based delivery of goods and services. Under such situations, poor quality of app may force customer to even pay slightly higher to competitor rather than putting efforts on poor-quality app.

Table 3.6 Chi-Square Test of Sampled Data

Sl. No.	Table Number	Computed Chi-Square	Value of P	Significance of Result	Outcome	Overall Outcome
1.	Table 1	134.7567	<0.00001	The result is significant at $P < 0.05$	Null hypothesis is rejected **in favor** of alternate hypothesis	The missing nonfunctional requirements impact the business success of both developing firms and client firms.
2.	Table 2	156.5313	<0.00001	The result is significant at $P < 0.05$	Null hypothesis is rejected **in favor** of alternate hypothesis	
3.	Table 3	134.7567	<0.00001	The result is significant at $P < 0.05$	Null hypothesis is rejected **in favor** of alternate hypothesis	
4.	Table 4	164.5985	<0.00001	The result is significant at $P < 0.05$	Null hypothesis is rejected **in favor** of alternate hypothesis	
5.	Table 5	164.5985	<0.00001	The result is significant at $P < 0.05$	Null hypothesis is rejected **in favor** of alternate hypothesis	

- High dissatisfaction will be so bad that the company may be out of the business forever in the same and other related products that is being offered by the firm.

This means that there is a strong relation between the number of missing NFRs and business success. However, the missing functional requirements are always bad for business success since missing requirement means missing utility of the app.

3.7 Threat to Validity

There are many parameters of business success and failures that could be employed to further study the impact of missing NFRs. Sample size is good enough but is aggregate of small, medium and large firms. The impact of missing NFRs may not be at the same level of damage for all these categories of firms but having same direction, i.e. positive correlation between number of missing NFRs and business success. The level of impact and comparative degree of damage will be interesting to watch.

3.8 Conclusion

Missing functional requirements is always bad for any business as it makes the software unusable. But, missing NFRs irrespective of how many functional requirements are implemented also makes the software unusable. This impacts developing firm business due to loss in reputation, financial losses in terms of free implementation of missing requirements, etc. On the other hand, missing NFRs makes it hard to reach potential customer of client firm. It may make them difficult to retain the customer, and any mistake in effective delivery of good/service through the developed app will make customer inclined towards the competitor. It is very hard to regain support of lost customer as claimed by one of the representatives. The final result if loss of revenue, losses and high probability to run out of business.

Chapter 4

Status of Nonfunctional Requirement in Mobile Application Development: An Empirical Study*

4.1 Introduction

The software industry aims to develop high-quality software for its clients under various development constraints. Huge expenditure is involved in undertaking a software project with likely failure risks threatening potential expected benefits.

The ability of a software to satisfy the customer results in an enhanced customer base, implying higher software sales and a good turnover. The reverse

---

* This article titled "**Status of Nonfunctional Requirements in Mobile Application Development: An Empirical Study**", appears in **Journal of Information Technology Research (JITR) (ISSN 1938-7857; eISSN 1938-7865),** Vol 10, Issue 1, **Copyright 2017, IGI Global,** www.igi-global.com. **Reprinted by permission of the publisher.**

of this situation negates the justification of investment in huge development costs. Failure not only results in a monetary loss in the current project but may also impact company's reputation thereby decreasing the customer base for future projects to be undertaken by the firm. Customer satisfaction is detrimental to the company's future.

Satisfaction comes from the ability of the software to meet the expectation of its customers/users. These customers are mainly concerned with the functionality of the software, i.e., functional requirements (FRs) of the software and hence nonfunctional ones are unseen initially.

However, if the same nonfunctional requirement (NFR) remains unimplemented, the FRs may become obsolete as they may be unable to deliver without nonfunctional areas or may be unusable till nonfunctional components are implemented.

Thus, the neglecting NFRs may lead to complete the rejection of the software among the stakeholders/customers although they were never called for directly.

In the case of mobile software development, various challenges get mapped to various NFRs like GUI, interactions with a large number of other apps, location awareness services, security, hardware and software independence apart from other traditional challenges such as usability, performance and reliability. The software developer must consider these issues in the form of NFRs during the development of the mobile apps. These issues can never be predefined and in fact depend on the level of expertise of the software developer.

For example, a software developer must consider the issues of database consistency as mobile networks usually perform handoffs. In the case of availability of a high-speed network, it is possible to increase the data transfer speed during transaction execution, thereby making consistency issues one of the more important NFRs. The successful implementation of the mobile app depends on the ability of a software developer to implement not only FR but also NFR by anticipating future events led by technological changes, environmental changes etc.

Numerous techniques are available to elicit software requirements and to prioritize these requirements. The available techniques focus mainly on FR available in the literature and very little work is available that handles NFRs separately or at least relative to FRs.

Keeping in view the importance of NFR in successful implementation of projects, especially mobile apps, the need was felt to undertake the survey of existing mobile app developments from the viewpoint of NFR contributions.

An effort is made to analyze the contribution of NFRs to the success/ failure rates of the product, analyze the status of NFRs, implementation and its contributions to the cost and time of overall development. Efforts are made to analyze the variation with an increase in the size of organization and complexity of the projects.

4.2 Motivation

The challenges in mobile app development can be mapped to different NFRs. NFRs determine the success or failure of projects. It is interesting to analyze the contribution of NFRs in the overall project from the historical data, ongoing live projects and industrial experience of mobile software developers. The outcome of the screening will motivate the researchers to consider NFRs equivalent to FRs.

4.3 Research Aim, Objective, Outcome

The aim of this research is to explore the relationship of NFRs with the undertaken mobile software project metrics, especially the cost, time, success rates and failure rates. The study also aims to identify and explain the various process models employed in software organizations in prioritizing the NFRs.

The objective was achieved through the following steps:

1. A survey conducted through the means of questionnaires with 13 developers from four development organizations. This formed the industrial survey. The outcome is both quantitative and qualitative.
2. A case study of a few mobile app projects undertaken and those ongoing in industries. This case study is Industrial Case Study.
3. Literature survey to gain deeper insights into the definitions of success rates, failure rates, existing prioritization techniques. The literature survey is an exploratory research to get familiar with the variable terms the study of which is a prime interest to this book.
4. Data analysis by comparison of surveys and case studies at different levels:
   - Level 1: analysis of data collected for case study and survey. These two empirical methods are studied separately and not in relation to each other.
   - Level 2: comparison of survey findings with case study findings.
   - Level 3: comparison of survey, case study and literature findings.

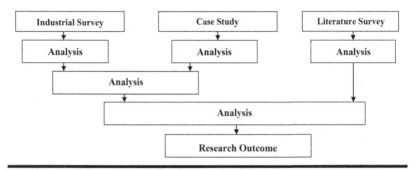

Figure 4.1 Research method.

Figure 4.1 presents the research method employed to answer the research questions forming the aim of research undertaken in this chapter.

The case study is undertaken in the form of analysis of historical documents and personal observation to verify, validate and/or add more to the analysis information of the industrial project survey. The advantage is that the researchers will get the opportunity to see if the practice adopted by survey participants is industry specific or generally followed across many firms. Further, the wrong or misleading information (if any) reported by industry participants either to hide some information as per company policy or support company vision policy or might be due to different terminologies used across different development firms (if any) will be minimized as a result of observations through the case studies. Case study undertaken by the researchers has given them the opportunity to verify the insight brought up by the survey participant with the things observed by the researchers.

4.4 Research Question

RQ 1. What is the extent to which nonfunctional requirements get the attention of software developers?

RQ 2. What is the cost and time percentage of NFR in the overall project cost and duration?

RQ 3. What is the implementation status of NFR to FR for different complexity projects?

RQ 4. What are the typical categories of NFRs implemented by mobile software developers?

RQ 5. How are nonfunctional requirements prioritized?

RQ 6. **What is the extent to which the answers to the above questions depend on the maturity and size of the software organization?**

RQ 7. **How the present practices of the mobile development firms impact project success and failure rates?**

4.5 Industrial Survey

The mobile software industry is generating mobile solutions for automating the solution generation for a variety of problems. The new branch of software engineering called mobile software engineering has emerged that deals with generating quality mobile applications. In order to get answers to the posted research questions (RQ 1–RQ 5) in the preceding section, a total of four software development firms are considered for data collection. The collected data were both qualitative and quantitative in nature.

The interviews and questionnaires were selected as possible data collection instruments or methods. A total of 12 participants from four firms (4 each from two companies, 3 from a third company and 1 from another firm) participated in the survey. These participants had experience of many projects and hence the data about many projects were collected from each developer. The developers were asked to give answers to questions asked by recalling the informative data for different complexity projects for different types of developments. The software was classified into low, medium and high complexity in accordance with the number of requirements and lines of code implemented.

The types of development include incremental development and "One-Go" technique. The objective is to see if the answers to research questions depend on development strategy or not. The details of the number of projects and representatives are given in Table 4.1.

The characteristics of the multinational mobile development organizations and the projects are given in Table 4.2.

The responses were collected from the industry participants to get answers to the research questions framed earlier. The responses collected for each research question are discussed next:

RQ 1. **What is the extent to which nonfunctional requirements get the software developers' attraction?**

The mobile applications should address a suitable number of NFRs because such applications are more constrained by characteristics such as network,

Table 4.1 Project Details

Sl. No.	Organization	Number of Representatives	Number of Project Experiences	Remarks
1.	A	04	29	Two developers had experience with the development of 10 projects and the remaining two had experience of 6 and 3.
2.	B	04	13	The developers had experience with 5, 3, 3 and 2 projects.
3.	C	03	7	The developers had experience with 2, 2 and 3 projects.
4.	D	01	2	The developer had experience with 2 projects.

operating environments, different expectations of users as compared to those with desktop applications and interactions with other apps (https:// sachinsdate.wordpress.com/2013/04/27/non-functional-requirements-in-mobile-applications/). These apps are to be used anywhere and anytime which implies the need for effective security. The operations of such apps are bound by the restrictions imposed by underlying hardware or development environment selected for implementation. The application will not be of any use if any of the important NFRs is dropped for implementation. For example, the application will be of no use if it takes a long time to get loaded on mobile browsers. The simple "performance" NFRs had made the application a failure.

Under the above-stated circumstances, any mobile developer can be expected to be more focused on NFRs or at least in balance with functional ones. The data reported by the interviewed representatives are quite surprising. The data are reported next with respect to different types of developments for different complexity of projects.

Table 4.2 Multinational Companies and Project Details

Sl. No.	Organization	Software Engineers Employed	Type of Project Development	No. of Projects	Product Complexity
1.	A	10,000+	Incremental	13	L, M, H
			One-go	12	L, M, H
			Mass-market incremental	04	H
2.	B	5000+	Incremental	6	L, M, H
			One-go	2	L, M, H
			Mass-market incremental	5	H
3.	C	50–100	Incremental	3	L, M, H
			One-go	4	L, M, H
4.	D	Below 50	Incremental	1	L, M, H
			One-go	1	L, M, H

■ Mass-market incremental development: in mass-market development, the focus is on the delivery of competitive features as early as possible. Limited time and unknown customer base make it difficult to take customers in confidence about NFRs. Further, limited time and the presence of competition in the market make the software developer less inclined toward NFRs. One of the industry representatives replied as *"A non functional requirement is of no use in tight schedule development in the competitive market as the customer never pays for non functional requirements"*. Incremental development makes it possible for the industry to justify the delay of implementation of NFRs in terms of the tight schedule, unknown market trends preferences etc. The few important nonfunctional features required for FRs to perform and those offered by competitive products are prime targets for such companies. In the early stages, the focus on NFRs is less, so as to reduce the development cost (and hence the price of the app) although as an organization makes its presence in markets, some important NFRs are implemented but customers are required to pay a price for them.

Company representatives told researchers that a mass mark product is always a high-complexity product, although it evolves from low complexity.

■ Bespoke development (incremental and one-go): in bespoke development, the clients are available for discussions. The development is made for known clients and hence the customer base is well known to both clients and developers. It is possible to interact with limited known clients/customers and convince them about a few important NFRs. The customers are unable to understand the NFRs and it is hard to convince them about it due to the increased costs and timelines. Thus, fewer important NFRs may be offered as free add-on features to them. The industries normally inform the customers about the extra charges of implementation of a few more NFRs in the future. However, in incremental developments, industries keep some margin in the price offered to clients and actual expected development cost. This is to cover the cost of implementation as add-on features. As understanding of NFRs gets enhanced during later increments and hence the client may be convinced for such NFRs at lower costs, marginal cost is employed to partly cover the complete cost. The existence of pressure of competitors and communication of clients with many competitors does not allow the developers to consider the NFRs as they will only add to cost and time rather than attracting customers about its functionality. One-go technique normally includes NFRs as a free add-on feature while incremental involves implementation in later increments by partly paying through cost margin. The procedure is similar for any complexity project, although a few extra NFRs are added to high-complexity project, a lot of effort is to be made with clients for this to happen.

RQ 2. What is the cost and time percentage of NFR in overall project cost and duration?

Industry participants told researchers that in case either of the two developments, the number of NFRs depends on the development time in hand and money invested by the client. If the development has large time and money, the number of NFRs is somewhat higher (although less) than those in a tight schedule and financially constrained projects. Industry participants also reported that it is most likely that every project is tightly scheduled and financially constrained. From the data presented by the industry participants, the percentage share of NFRs in total cost and development time of the project is as given next:

- Mass-market incremental projects: the percentage share of NFRs in cost is on average 8% of the total cost and 19% of total time. Low cost is attributable to less number of NFRs being implemented and 19% time-share means that NFRs take a lot of time to get implemented.
- Bespoke incremental:
  - Low complexity: the cost share is 2% of the total cost and the time-share is 3% of total development time.
  - Medium complexity: the cost share is 3% of the total cost and time is 5% of the total time.
  - Large complexity: the cost share is 4% and time-share of 6%.
- Bespoke one-go:
  - Low complexity: the cost share is 2% and time-share is 4%.
  - Medium complexity: the cost share is 3% and time-share of 4%.
  - Large complexity: the cost share is 3% and time-share of 5%.

The data present some important and interesting figures. The cost and time values are higher for mass-market developments because these are undertaken by large organizations that are matured enough in adopted practices and experiences. These organizations undertake high-complexity projects. Such organizations are more influenced by market turbulences.

The low values of cost and time-share in bespoke one-go technique are due to the fact that in such projects, the clients are hard to convince about the NFRs, which is mostly implemented as add-on free services. Free services mean that only the important ones (too less in number) are offered by organizations. Further, for medium- and high/large-complexity projects, the cost share is similar although time-share differs. This is because, in the case of high-complexity project, the number of FRs increases, thereby requiring the developer to have a sound understanding about the other requirements to be implemented for successful implementation of nonfunctional ones. Time percentage increases with increase in project complexity.

For bespoke incremental projects, the cost and time-share is almost similar to bespoke one-go ones. The cost and time increases with an increase in complexity like in the one-go technique. The values given previously are average values of both matured and nonmatured projects. For example, a cost of 3% and time 5% for bespoke incremental medium-complexity project is computed by adding the cost and time values of all medium-complexity projects of both matured and less matured organizations.

The averaged data were shown to the industry participants to get them verified. The reason was that individual data was not available and the estimate was rough estimate. During the verification process, industry participants raised one important trend. The values of cost and time-share for bespoke development of different complexity projects are lower for well-established organizations than less matured ones. The reason is the different experiences, knowledge of developers and maturity level of the organizations.

The cost and time data were very hard for the participants to share because the project development is not a one-man affair and the same person is not involved in every phase of development. However, the industry participants were able to gather the data from documentations, bills and interactions with finance departments. Fewer participants were not able to supply any data due to lacking documentation and high staff turnover. For incremental projects, the cost and time data are supplied as an average of increment values. The values of starting increment to the most stable increment (customers' requests diminish and products become older) are averaged to arrive at the project cost and time.

RQ 3. What is the implementation status of NFR to FR for different complexity projects?

The gathering of NFRs and their selection is done by developers alone. Customers do not have any understanding of these requirements. They are concerned with cost, time and functionality of the software. Developers freeze the FRs for particular increment or as per the agreed software cost for one-go technique. Thereafter, the developers start deciding the NFRs required by the application to support FRs. These NFRs are never subjected to requirement prioritization along with FRs. The FRs are prioritized separately. The NFRs are never subjected to prioritization. Nonimplementation of potential NFRs is argued by a few developers that customers want FRs and are ready to pay for them only. One of the developers said that the nonhandling of NFRs saves man-hours (cost or effort) and time that can be invested for FRs.

The ratio of the number of NFRs to FRs increases as one moves from bespoke to mass-market development from complexity of low to high. The increase is not high as compared to FRs. Typical ratios are given in Table 4.3.

RQ 4. What are the typical categories of NFRs implemented by mobile software developers?

There do not exist any well-defined categories of NFRs in the industries. The NFRs are invented by looking at the FRs as agreed with the customers.

**Table 4.3   NFR to FR Ratios for Different Categories and
Complexity Projects**

Sl. No.	Project Development	Product Complexity	NFR to FR (Less Matured To Matured Range)
1.	Mass-market incremental	High	0.15 nearly
	Bespoke incremental	High	0.16–0.21
		Medium	0.23–0.29
1.		Low	0.32–0.35
3.	Bespoke one-go	High	0.22–0.26
		Medium	0.25–0.30
		Low	0.26–0.32

The invention is also based on the offerings or mistakes made by the competitors (for mass-market developments). However, the typical NFRs as reported by the industry participants are those related to performance (including optimalism), reliability, security, availability, usability, responsiveness, GUI requirements and storage. Requirements such as platform independence and context awareness are rarely considered by them because they are costly and time-consuming.

RQ 5. How are nonfunctional requirements prioritized?

The NFRs are not subjected to any prioritization. It is the experience of the developer that made him think about the typically required NFRs and the ones that are mandatory. The developer must convince both the management and customer about the need for the NFR and push them for the same. The developer must search the reusable code for the NFR so that the cost and time is greatly reduced. One reason for this includes the ignorance of management and hence nonsanction of finance for the NFR. NFRs must steal a little amount from the funds sectioned for FRs for their implementation. The prioritization is not there for any complexity project belonging to any type of development. However, efforts made by developer for identifying NFR are larger for mass-market product than incremental bespoke products, with minimal for one-go technique product. The effort increases by switching from bespoke to the mass market with the complexity of the product due to the increase in the potential NFR that may support large number of FRs.

RQ 6. What is the extent to which the answers to the above questions depend on the maturity and size of software organization?

Software organizations vary in terms of their size and maturity. Organizations that are matured enough (large sized) are involved in all types of development, i.e., mass market and bespoke (for example, customization). However, less matured organizations with small or medium size are normally involved in bespoke developments. The market developments are confined to well-known market segments, but as the segments are not well distributed globally, they are termed as bespoke in this book.

In the case of the matured large organizations, there is availability of experience of previous projects and reusable codes. The finance is available and to satisfy the vision of the organization, these companies may go for fewer NFRs as free features or may implement them at lower costs due to reuse of experience and code. These organizations sacrifice their profits for the first few increments and cover them in other projects or later increments. The effort is to enlarge customer base and increase in reputation. For example, a situation could arise where the new project can be undertaken with maximum reusability possible. In such cases, the new project may give newly recruited engineers an opportunity to gain experience with seniors. Thus, even less profit is earned but there is enough gain in experience of available engineers that will be fruitful in later projects.

Small-sized, less matured organizations are forced to offer these NFRs as a free add-on feature or delay necessary feature for later increments where they can be charged.

The time and cost of implementation is higher than those with matured organizations, but the number of NFRs is smaller. Higher comparative value is due to the presence of less experience and reusability options. The number of NFRs is very little in comparison to functional ones, but well-matured organizations implement NFRs higher than those in small organizations.

The ratio of the number of NFR to FR is higher for matured organizations than those for less matured ones but the difference is not too much. For example, a matured organization involved in the delivery of high-complexity projects using bespoke incremental will have higher ratio than those of less matured organizations.

The value of the ratio is higher for low-complexity projects and gets lowered for high-complexity projects for both types of organizations for any development type. Lowering of the ratio does not mean that high-complexity projects do not have increased NFRs, but it means that the increase is not comparable to increase in FRs. The decrease in ratio with the increase in complexity is not too steep for matured ones than less matured ones.

The matured organizations implement the previously implemented NFRs in new similar projects along with those offered by competitors.

In the case of less matured ones, the NFRs are the "common" requirements while matured ones may go one step higher with some innovative market nonfunctional features too. Innovativeness is higher in incremental than one-go developments. This means that ratio value is higher for incremental developments than those based on one-go technique. As stated earlier, the ratio decreases with the increase in complexity for particular development type. There is no prioritization of NFRs in any organizations.

RQ 7. How the present practices of the mobile development firms impact project success and failure rates?

Product success and project success are of different terms. A successful project may lead to unsuccessful product in the market and successful product in the market may be a result of failed projects (http://c2.com/cgi/wiki?DefinitionOfProjectFailure). One problem in defining the success is deciding the success metrics for project and product. Product success means that the product had been accepted by the customers. In the case of incremental products, the product must be able to retain old customers and attract new ones. The success is defined by the number of old and new customers. Continuously increasing customer base is a good signal of product success. Problems in costs (like over budget), time schedule (like late) and quality are the metrics for project success/failure and may or may not impact the customer base. The software is delivered to mass markets with unknown customers (early increments) to have known ones (in later increments) (Gupta et al., 2015c). A number of new requests and change requests are likely to increase and finally decrease. One measure of such incremental products is customer satisfaction or likes for the projects. To estimate the success or failure of the product, the following could be the ways:

■ Estimate the number of customers using the product sales data.
■ Estimate the number of customers by using sale data and update downloads. This considers the estimation of old customer which is still with the organization.

■ Apply transformation on own company data and competitor to make two projects comparable. The two company's projects may be different in cost, time and versions. After transformations, compare the sales of the two products to get an estimate of customer base for two projects. Many similar projects can be compared after applying the transformations.

Because the studies projects are incremental and developed as one-go product, the industry participants were asked to give the number of customers using any of the steps given earlier. The responsibility to calculate the number of customers was given to these participants. Participants were told about the possible ways of calculation so that they may get enough time to get quality estimates. The participants were reluctant in giving the exact number so they were asked to categorize them into three—low, medium and high. Participants were asked to specify the number of customers as estimated by marketing department and management. Participants were also asked to specify the categories of customer numbers that they believe reduced due to nonimplementation of NFRs. The increase in customers means that NFRs do not impact success rates, participants were asked to specify this situation as "No Effect". For matured organizations, the data are reported in customer number and change in customer columns of Table 4.4, quick averaging performed to get single representative value.

The data reported by the companies organized against the maturity of the firms are given in Table 4.4.

Table 4.4 shows that matured organizations involved in mass-market development are impacted by nonimplementation of NFRs, although the effect is not on high scale because of good management practices. However, they are able to satisfy the customers better in bespoke incremental projects because of known customers and ability to implement them in next increment as competitors are missing from scenario for current undertaken project only. The organizations are able to perform better in one-go development as fixed customers are known before development and a good number of basic NFRs go in implementation. Matured organizations take a lead for one-go technique because a number of NFRs implemented are larger than those by less matured organizations.

The findings of the industrial survey are presented in Table 4.5.

Table 4.4 Effect of NFR on Product Success

Sl. No.	Type of Company	Development Type	Customer Number	Change in Customer Number (Decrease due to NFR)	Stated Reason
1.	Matured	Mass-market incremental	High	Medium	High competition. Any obsolete feature provides competitor a chance. However, good management is losing point to the competitors.
		Bespoke incremental	High	Low	Ability to understand known customers. Less effect of competitor on undertaken project. Possibility to improve the code in later increments.
		Bespoke one-go	High	Low (very low)	Important functional requirements implemented.
2.	Less matured	Bespoke incremental	High and medium	Medium	Impact of lack of experience and poor project management.
		Bespoke one-go	Low	Low	Particular clients and known customers give the organization an ability to understand NFRs.

Table 4.5   Industrial Survey Results

Sl. No.	Research Question	Project Development and Complexity	Remarks
1.	RQ 1. What is the extent to which nonfunctional requirements get the software developers' attraction?	Mass-market incremental	Little attention is paid. Customers need to pay for nonfunctional requirements.
		Bespoke incremental	Marginal cost used to pay partly for nonfunctional requirements.
		Bespoke one-go	Offered as free add-on feature.
2.	RQ 2. What is the cost and time percentage of NFR in overall project cost and duration?	Mass-market incremental (high)	Cost percentage is 8% of total cost and 19% of total time.
		Bespoke incremental (low, med, high)	Cost percentage is in range of 2–4% total cost and 3–6% of total time.
		Bespoke one-go (low, med, high)	Cost percentage is in range of 2–3% total cost and 4–5% of total time.
3.	RQ 3. What is the implementation status of NFR to FR for different complexity projects?	Mass-market incremental Bespoke incremental Bespoke one-go	Higher ratio for matured organization than less matured organization values. The ratio decreases from one-go bespoke to mass-market incremental.

4.	RQ 4. What are the typical categories of NFRs implemented by mobile software developer?	Mass-market incremental Bespoke incremental Bespoke one-go	No well-defined category. It depends on cost, time and functional requirements. Typical NFR includes performance (including optimalism), reliability, security, availability, usability, responsiveness, GUI requirements and storage.
5.	RQ 5. How are nonfunctional requirements prioritized?	Mass-market incremental Bespoke incremental Bespoke one-go	They are not subjected to any prioritization. They are invented by developer in accordance with what his experience says.
6.	RQ 6. What is the extent to which the answers to the above questions depend on the maturity and size of software organization?	Matured large organizations	• NFRs considered to some extent. Innovativeness is mostly in incremental ones. One-go developments witness almost previously implemented ones. • Low costs and time of NFR implementations. • Ratio of NFR to FR decreases with increase in complexity but decrease not steep. Values are higher for mass market than bespoke incremental and bespoke one-go.
		Less matured small organizations	• NFRs are implemented with higher costs and time. • Offer NFR as free add-on or charged ones in later increments. • Ratio of NFR to FR decreases from low to high complexity and relative decrease is higher than matured ones. • Ratio value is smaller in one-go than incremental.

(Continued)

Table 4.5 **Industrial Survey Results (*Continued*)**

Sl. No.	Research Question	Project Development and Complexity	Remarks
7.	RQ 7. How the present practices of the mobile development firms impact project success and failure rates?	Matured organizations	• High impact in mass-market developments although good management keep dropout rate to medium. • Better understanding of customers and absence of competitor in bespoke (once project is allotted), option to implement in later increments lowers the dropout rate of customers. • For one-go, NFRs are almost all basic and few more and customers are well known, so dropout rate is too low.
		Less matured organizations	• Poor management and less NFR implementation make dropout rate to medium.

4.6 Case Study

In order to validate the data reported by industry representatives, the researchers had undertaken a case study with a few mobile app developing firms. Three types of firms were selected—small, medium and large—to get involved in bespoke development (incremental and one-go) and mass-market development. There could be many data collection strategies in the case study as suggested in Yim (1993) but the analysis of literature and other documents and observation on ongoing development activity, especially requirements engineering, made answering the posted research questions possible. The documentations may be outdated, inconsistent and may not have complete data regarding the financial information. It made it necessary to analyze other available development-related documents. The data collection strategies used for answering the research questions are given in Table 4.6.

The observations made for each research question are as follows.

RQ 1. What is the extent to which nonfunctional requirements get the software developers' attraction?

The projects undertaken by industries run from highly unstructured, formal ways to more structured, formal ways with increase in both complexity and the nature of the development. In the case of bespoke one-go technique, only those features are delivered that are agreed to with the clients. Agreeing means that clients have agreed to the functionality that will be delivered and also development costs and estimated time schedule. Clients never agree to

Table 4.6 Research Questions and Case Study Data Collection Strategies

Sl. No.	Research Question	Data Collection Strategy
1.	RQ 1	Documentations, observations of ongoing development activities and interviews.
2.	RQ 2	Other documents.
3.	RQ 3	Documentations.
4.	RQ 4	Documentations and observations of ongoing development activities.
5.	RQ 5	Documentations, observations of ongoing development activities and interviews.

NFRs due to lack of clarity, increased costs, dropping a few FRs to adjust NFRs and increased time schedule.

In the case of bespoke incremental technique, the developers are in somewhat a relaxed mode as any missing requirement can be delivered later on. Any error in estimations will be adjusted in later increments. Clients sometimes agree to implementation of NFRs, but the number is limited to very little. Further, if any NFR is missing, it may make FRs obsolete, and in later increments, it can be considered as a new request of the highest priority. Sometimes, marginal costs or extra payments are used to implement these NFRs. Extra payments are also possible in case the clients understand the importance of the missing requirements.

In the case of mass-market products, developers do focus on few NFRs that are essential for project success. The software is purchased on its ability to deliver the functionality at lower cost and time as compared to the competitor. The time to market and cost are considered as prime attributes for delivering innovative, functional features, thereby making sound reasons for less focus of developers on NFRs which happen to be time-consuming and costly.

RQ 2. What is the cost and time percentage of NFR in overall project cost and duration?

A number of NFRs are lesser in bespoke projects than in mass-market incremental development. The cost and time varies in accordance with the experience of the developers, size of organization etc. Bigger organizations have less time for undertaking implementation of NFRs of complex projects due to availability of reusable code or previous experience. However, the limited number of NFRs results in its lesser percentage share in total cost and development time. An increase in the number of NFRs will increase the cost and time-share because as requirements are costly and time-consuming to implement. The empirical cost and time of previous projects (average) is as given as follows:

- Mass-market incremental projects: cost varies between 8 and 12% and time from 10 to 18% with minimal time for well-established organizations and higher for small- or medium-sized companies.
- Bespoke incremental:
  - Low complexity: the cost share is a range of 2–3% to the total cost and time-share is 3–4% of total development time.
  - Medium complexity: the cost share is 2–4% of the total cost and time is 2–5% of total time.
  - Large complexity: the cost share is 4–6% and 4–8% is time-share.

■ Bespoke one-go:
  – Low complexity: the cost share is 1–2% and time-share is 3–4%.
  – Medium complexity: the cost share is 1–3% and time-share is 4–6%.
  – Large complexity: the cost share is roughly 3 and 5% time-share.

RQ 3. What is the implementation status of NFR to FR for different complexity projects?

The number of NFRs in industrial projects is almost negligible as compared to FRs. But if still compared, the ratio comes out to be 0.15–0.20 for low complexity, 0.13–0.16 for medium and 0.11–0.13 for high-complexity projects. The decrease in the ratio is because, with the increase in complexity of projects, the increase in the number of FRs is not linear with the increase in the number of NFRs.

The number of NFRs increases, but not as much as the increase in FRs. Higher ratios are for well-established organizations. The ratios decrease as we move from low to high complexity, but the decrease is not very pronounced. It means that these organizations have little focus on NFRs and more on the functional ones.

Typical ratios are given in Table 4.7.

RQ 4. What are the typical categories of NFRs implemented by mobile software developers?

Developers keep focusing on the nonfunctional ones delivered by competitors and those they have implemented in earlier projects. The effort is to reuse the existing code to the maximum possible extent. The innovative nonfunctional features required are handled by a group of experts with one expert and few beginners to manage time and cost.

Table 4.7 NFR to FR Ratios for Different Categories and Complexity Projects

Sl. No.	Product Complexity	NFR to FR Ratio
1.	Low	0.15–0.20
2.	Medium	0.13–0.16
3.	High	0.11–0.13

RQ 5. How are nonfunctional requirements prioritized?

Industries have limited NFRs that are to be implemented within time and budget constraints. Prioritization involves huge costs and time and because the number is limited so no prioritization practices take place.

RQ 6. What is the extent to which the answers to the above questions depend on the maturity and size of software organization?

The researchers had observed various complexity projects of different types of organizations as follows:

- Mass-market incremental development—small and medium (less matured) and large companies. The project belongs to high complexity only.
- Bespoke incremental—all complexity projects of small and medium (less matured) and matured large companies.
- Bespoke one-go—all complexity projects of small and medium (less matured) and large matured companies.

The mass-market development will involve high-complexity projects only. Large companies are matured companies and will be involved in all type types of developments of all complexity projects. Small and medium companies will be less matured and involved in bespoke developments of projects of different complexities.

Matured organizations involved in any type of development focus on NFRs to maintain competitive edge and implement the vision policies. But the number of NFRs is very less as compared to functional. Organizations expertise and matured engineering principles help them implement NFRs in less cost and time. However, with increase in complexity, the ratio of the number of NFRs to functional decreases. The cost and time is less in bespoke than mass market because in bespoke incremental, the organizations get enough time understanding the project dynamisms. Sometimes, the customer realizes the importance of NFRs and gets ready to pay. Sometimes, the parallel projects or code given to student interns gives organizations the cost-effective solution to the implementation problem. The parameters for matured organizations are better than those in less matured ones.

RQ 7. How the present practices of the mobile development firms impact project success and failure rates?

The data were difficult to collect and present here. The reason was that the companies were reluctant in sharing project information; there was no access to old projects; the success of product and project was ambiguous terms. However, informal talks with the organization yielded below-mentioned observations:

- Increase in project complexity for the same development type makes the impact of missing NFR on product success hard. This is due to widening of scope and need for more NFRs.
- Moving from bespoke one-go to bespoke incremental and finally to mass market increases the impact.
- Matured organizations are better placed in terms of product success than small/medium organizations due to better experiences of developers and good project management.

An increase in the customer base leads to an increase in a number of requirements. If enough NFRs are selected, then the project success rate will increase. However, it is actually functional ones that determine the sale prospective of such software.

The findings of the case study are presented in Table 4.8:

4.7 Comparative Analysis

As discussed in previous sections, the research method involves the analysis of the collected data at various levels given as follows:

- Level 1: analysis of data collected for case study and survey. These two empirical methods are studied separately and not in relation to each other.
- Level 2: comparison of survey findings with case study findings.
- Level 3: comparison of survey, case study and literature findings.

Level 1 is completed in preceding sections. The industrial projects' findings are compared to the case study results to complete Level 2 of the analysis. The comparative results are given in Table 4.9.

The data analyzed through comparative analysis of industrial projects and case study observations converged into common agreement. The empirical results agreed with each other, meaning the data reported by industry participants and the students are prevailing in real industrial situations. The

Table 4.8   Case Study Findings

Sl. No.	Research Question	Project Development and Complexity	Remarks
1.	RQ 1. What is the extent to which nonfunctional requirements get the software developers' attraction?	Mass-market incremental	Fewer NFRs implemented. Effort is to enhance success rates in competitive markets.
		Bespoke incremental	Marginal cost and payments used to implement NFRs. Clients can be slightly convinced for the same.
		Bespoke one-go	Offered as free add-on feature. Clients can never be convinced.
2.	RQ 2. What is the cost and time percentage of NFR in overall project cost and duration?	Mass-market incremental (high)	Cost varies between 8 and 12% and time from 10 to 18%. Lower rates are there for well-established bigger organizations.
		Bespoke incremental (low, med, high)	Cost share of 2–6% and time 3–8%. High-complexity projects have higher cost and time-share. Range varies according to maturity and organization size.
		Bespoke one-go (low, med, high)	Cost percentage is in range of 1–3% of the total cost and 3–5% of the total time.

3.	RQ 3. What is the implementation status of NFR to FR for different complexity projects?	Mass-market incremental, bespoke incremental, bespoke one-go	The ratio comes out to be 0.15–0.20 for low complexity, 0.13–0.16 for medium and 0.11–0.13 for high-complexity projects. Decrease in ratio is higher for high-complexity projects because of increase in number of functional requirements than NFRs. Ratio decrease is slight less for matured organizations.
4.	RQ 4. What are the typical categories of NFRs implemented by mobile software developers?	Mass-market incremental Bespoke incremental Bespoke one-go	No well-defined category. It depends on competitor, previously implemented NFRs, reusability aspect and innovativeness (mass market only).
5.	RQ 5. How are nonfunctional requirements prioritized	Mass-market incremental Bespoke incremental Bespoke one-go	They are not subjected to any prioritization. Prioritization is considered as a biggest reason for increase in cost and timeline.
6.	RQ 6. What is the extent to which the answers to the above questions depend on the maturity and size of software organization?	Matured organizations	• Better ratio of NFR to FR. • Ratio decreases from one-go to incremental. • Ratio decreases with increase in project complexity. • Time and cost is higher in mass market than bespoke incremental and one-go. • Time and cost for any development type and complexity better than corresponding values for less matured ones. • Innovative NFR can be implemented due to possibility of reuse. • No prioritization employed.

(Continued)

Table 4.8 Case Study Findings (*Continued*)

Sl. No.	Research Question	Project Development and Complexity	Remarks
		Less matured organizations	• NFR's financial burden mostly on customers. • Ratio decreases from one-go to incremental. • Ratio decreases with increase in project complexity. • Time and cost is higher in mass market than bespoke incremental and one-go. • Time and cost less than those with matured ones. • Basic NFR implemented.
7.	RQ7. How the present practices of the mobile development firms impact project success and failure rates?	Matured organizations	• Impact of missing NFR hard on product success with increase in complexity. • Good management practices make impact up to maximum level of dropout rate to medium.
		Less matured organizations	• Impact increases with increase in complexity but increase higher than in the case of matured ones.

Table 4.9 Comparative Results of Industrial and Case Study Results

Sl. No.	Research Question	Project Development and Complexity	Industrial Survey Analysis Results	Case Study Observations	Comparative Results (Y for Consistent)
1.	RQ 1. What is the extent to which nonfunctional requirements get the software developers' attraction?	Mass-market incremental	Little attention is paid. Customers need to pay for nonfunctional requirements.	Fewer NFRs implemented. The effort is to enhance success rates in competitive markets.	
		Bespoke incremental	Marginal cost used to pay partly for nonfunctional requirements.	Marginal cost and payments used to implement NFRs. Clients can be slightly convinced for the same.	Y
		Bespoke one-go	Offered as a free add-on feature.	Offered as a free add-on feature. Clients can never be convinced.	Y

(Continued)

Table 4.9   Comparative Results of Industrial and Case Study Results (*Continued*)

Sl. No.	Research Question	Project Development and Complexity	Industrial Survey Analysis Results	Case Study Observations	Comparative Results (Y for Consistent)
2.	RQ 2. What is the cost and time percentage of NFR in overall project cost and duration?	Mass-market incremental (high)	Cost percentage is 8% of the total cost and 19% of the total time.	The cost varies between 8 and 12% and time from 10 to 18%. Lower rates are there for well-established bigger organizations.	Y
		Bespoke incremental (low, med, high)	Cost percentage is in the range 2–4% of the total cost and 3–6% of the total time.	Cost share of 2–6% and time 3–8%. High complexity projects have higher cost and time-share. Range varies among maturity and organization size.	Y
		Bespoke one-go (low, med, high)	Cost percentage is in the range 2–3% total cost and 4–5% of total time.	Cost percentage is in the range of 1–3% of the total cost and 3–5% of the total time.	Y

| 3. | RQ 3. What is the implementation status of NFR to FR for different complexity projects? | Mass-market incremental, bespoke incremental, bespoke one-go. | Consolidated ratio is 0.15–0.26 for high, 0.23–0.30 for medium and 0.26–0.35 for low-complexity projects for bespoke and mass market. Ratio decreases from bespoke one-go to bespoke incremental and finally to mass-market developments. However, the decrease is higher for high-complexity projects. | The ratio comes out to be 0.15–0.20 for low complexity, 0.13–0.16 for medium and 0.11–0.13 for high complexity projects. Decrease in ratio is higher for high-complexity projects because of the increase in the number of functional requirements than NFRs. The ratio decrease is slightly less for matured organizations. | Y |

(Continued)

Table 4.9 Comparative Results of Industrial and Case Study Results (*Continued*)

Sl. No.	Research Question	Project Development and Complexity	Industrial Survey Analysis Results	Case Study Observations	Comparative Results (Y for Consistent)
4.	RQ 4. What are the typical categories of NFRs implemented by mobile software developers?	Mass-market incremental Bespoke incremental Bespoke one-go	No well-defined category. It depends on cost, time and functional requirements. Typical NFR includes performance (including optimalism), reliability, security, availability, usability, responsiveness, GUI requirements and storage.	No well-defined category. It depends on the competitor, previously implemented NFRs, reusability aspect and innovativeness (mass market only).	Y
5.	RQ 5. How are nonfunctional requirements prioritized?	Mass-market incremental Bespoke incremental Bespoke one-go	They are not subjected to any prioritization. They are invented by the developer in accordance with what his experience says.	• They are not subjected to any prioritization. Prioritization is considered as a big reason for increase in cost and timeline.	Y

					Y
6.	RQ 6. What is the extent to which the answers to the above questions depend on the maturity and size of software organization?	Matured large organizations	• NFRs considered to some extent. Innovativeness is mostly in incremental ones. One-go developments witness almost previously implemented ones. • Low costs and time of NFR implementations. • Ratio of NFR to FR decreases with the increase in complexity, but decrease not steep. Values are higher for mass market than bespoke incremental and bespoke one-go.	• Innovative NFR can be implemented due to possibility of reuse. • Better ratio of NFR to FR. • The ratio decreases from one-go to incremental. • The ratio decreases with increase in project complexity. • Time and cost is higher in mass market than bespoke incremental and one-go. • Time and cost for any development type and complexity better than corresponding values for less matured ones. • No prioritization employed.	

(Continued)

Table 4.9 Comparative Results of Industrial and Case Study Results (*Continued*)

Sl. No.	Research Question	Project Development and Complexity	Industrial Survey Analysis Results	Case Study Observations	Comparative Results (Y for Consistent)
		Less matured small organizations	• NFRs are implemented with higher costs and time. • Offer NFR as a free add-on or charged ones in later increments. • Ratio of NFR to FR decreases from low to high complexity and relative decrease is higher than matured ones. • Ratio value is smaller in one-go than incremental.	• NFRs have high costs and time associated. • NFR's financial burden mostly on customers. • The ratio decreases from one-go to incremental. • The ratio decreases with increase in project complexity. • Time and cost is higher in mass market than bespoke incremental and one-go. • Time and cost less than those with matured ones. • Basic NFR implemented.	Y

| 7. | RQ 7. How the present practices of the mobile development firms impact project success and failure rates? | Matured organizations Less matured organization | • The impact of missing NFR on project success increases with increase in project complexity and type of development (bespoke one-go to mass-market incremental).
 • The above trends hold in both matured and less matured firms but are less in matured firms. | • The impact of missing NFR hard on product success with an increase in complexity.
 • Impact increases with an increase in complexity, but increase higher than in the case of matured ones. | Y |

reported results are verified and validated through case studies. The agreed analysis is to be compared with the findings of the literature surveys. This final level of comparative analysis proceeds to identify the gaps between the research reported by researchers and those prevailing in industries. Table 4.9 gives the results of this comparative analysis.

4.7.1 Comparative Analysis of Survey Results, Case Study and Literature Survey

To complete Level 3 of the adopted research methodology (Figure 4.1), the results of industrial survey, case study and literature survey are compared and presented in Table 4.10. The literature survey had resulted in limited information about the research questions. However, the limited information and inferences applied made the comparative analysis possible. The comparative analysis is shown in Table 4.10. However, the comparison cannot be made at finer levels against different complexity and development types.

4.8 Conclusion

This chapter aimed to undertake different types of studies to achieve an understanding of the mobile software development from the perspective of NFRs. The software product success depends on its ability to satisfy both FR and NFR. NFRs are always neglected and considered in an ad hoc fashion and never with the same care as with which FRs are handled. To achieve this aim, the following types of studies like exploratory, descriptive and explanatory are conducted in industrial environment and published literature.

The case study, industrial survey and literature survey converged into common finding that NFRs are almost ignored by software industries and amount of consideration decreases from mass market to incremental and bespoke one-go technique. NFRs are not prioritized by the software industries and only rely on understanding of the developers. A fewer number of NFR are selected for implementation thereby making their less contribution to overall development cost but higher share in development time. Percentage shares in cost and time increase with increase in complexity of project and with as one moves from mass market to one-go development. Neglection of NFRs results in making the project success probabilistic. Matured organizations partially absorb the impact of missing NFRs which otherwise has a higher scale impact on small- and medium-size organizations. Continued ignorance of such requirements by matured organization in mass market will

Table 4.10 Comparative Results of Industrial Survey, Case Study and Literature Survey Results

Sl. No.	Research Question	Industrial Survey and Case Study Analysis Results	Literature Survey Results	Comparative Results (Y for Consistent)
1.	RQ 1. What is the extent to which nonfunctional requirements get the software developers' attraction?	Little attention is paid. Customers need to pay for nonfunctional requirements. Marginal cost used to pay partly for nonfunctional requirements. Alternatively offered as a free add-on feature.	There is a lack of available work in literature that highlights the manner the mobile app developers select the nonfunctional requirements for implementation. There is no agreement for NFRs to be implemented.	Yes (Y) but there is no evidence in the literature about how NFRs are implemented.
2.	RQ 2. What is the cost and time percentage of NFR in overall project cost and duration?	Cost and time is higher for mass-market incremental than bespoke incremental and bespoke one-go.	The overall implementation cost and time of nonfunctional requirements implemented by matured organizations would be smaller but larger than those developed by small or medium organizations.	Y

(Continued)

Table 4.10 Comparative Results of Industrial Survey, Case Study and Literature Survey Results (*Continued*)

Sl. No.	Research Question	Industrial Survey and Case Study Analysis Results	Literature Survey Results	Comparative Results (Y for Consistent)
3.	RQ 3. What is the implementation status of NFR to FR for different complexity projects?	Ratio value is smaller. Decrease in ratio is higher for high-complexity projects because of the increase in the number of functional requirements than NFRs. The ratio decrease is slightly less for matured organizations.	The ratio is higher for incremental projects implemented by large organization. It is smaller for typical one-go projects implemented by small or medium organizations.	Yes (Y). There is a difference between value of ratio for industrial projects and those disseminated in literature. Although difference is small.
4.	RQ 4. What are the typical categories of NFRs implemented by mobile software developers?	No well-defined category. It depends on cost, time and functional requirements. Innovative requirements implemented by matured organizations and traditional by others.	No well-defined category but most researchers settled various NFRs like look and feel, usability, performance, environmental, security, cultural requirements, reliability, battery consumption, availability, portability, scalability, maintainability and security.	Y

5.	RQ 5. How are nonfunctional Requirements prioritized?	They are not subjected to any prioritization. They are invented by the developer in accordance with what his experience says.	Literature survey does not result in extraction of any work related to prioritization of nonfunctional requirements.	Y
6.	RQ 6. What is the extent to which the answers to the above questions depend on the maturity and size of software organization?	• Matured organizations implemented somewhat large number of nonfunctional requirements. • Low costs and time of NFR implementations. • Ratio of NFR to FR decreases with the increase in complexity, but decrease not steep. Values are higher for mass market than bespoke incremental and bespoke one-go.	Maturity of organizations has an impact on the number of nonfunctional requirements in projects. The ratio is higher for incremental projects implemented by large organizations. It is smaller for typically one-go projects implemented by small or medium organizations. Variation of a number of such requirements with the change in complexity of the project is unknown phenomenon due to lack of information available in the literature.	Y

(Continued)

Table 4.10 Comparative Results of Industrial Survey, Case Study and Literature Survey Results (*Continued*)

Sl. No.	Research Question	Industrial Survey and Case Study Analysis Results	Literature Survey Results	Comparative Results (Y for Consistent)
7.	RQ 7. How the present practices of the mobile development firms impact project success and failure rates?	The impact of missing NFR on project success increases with increase in project complexity and type of development (bespoke one-go to mass-market incremental).	The work is not reported in the extracted papers.	Comparative analysis so far makes us believe that missing NFR will impact product success and impact depends on the complexity of the product, type of development and maturity of organizations.

throw such an organization out of the market. The conclusions for every six research questions on the basis of the comparatively agreed insights brought by various empirical methods are as follows.

RQ 1. What is the extent to which nonfunctional requirements get the software developers' attraction?

NFRs are the most ignored parts of the mobile software projects. Normally, the very basic NFRs made it to the implementation sets with some innovative and competitive NFRs likely seen in implementation sets of matured organizations, especially in incremental developments. The reason is that these organizations are big organizations with large database of reusable code and experience. To maintain a competitive edge, they are forced to implement innovative, FR and NFR. Higher costs and timeline due to less developer experience and development from scratch make small and medium organizations reluctant to the idea of the large number of NFRs.

RQ 2. What is the cost and time percentage of NFR in overall project cost and duration?

NFRs are costlier and take large time to get implemented. The contribution in total development cost and time is less due to less number of NFRs selected for implementation. However, the cost and time percentage does not increase rapidly in the incremental development of matured organizations, even though they implement large NFRs than those implemented by small or medium organizations. The cost and time percentage increases with increase in project complexity and with shift from small/medium-size organization to large organizations.

RQ 3. What is the implementation status of NFR to FR for different complexity projects?

A number of NFRs in projects are negligible as compared to functional projects. The ratio is higher for matured organizations in incremental projects than those implemented by less matured organization, but not too high. The ratio decreases with an increase in complexity of the project, but the decrease is less with the increase in maturity and size of organizations.

RQ 4. What are the typical categories of NFRs implemented by mobile software developers?

The NFRs are composed of many sub-NFRs. Some NFRs have functional aspects too.

In industrial projects, the NFRs range from basic to innovative, competitive ones. Researchers had reported fewer NFRs that include requirements like look and feel, usability, performance, environmental, security, cultural requirements, reliability, battery consumption, availability, portability, scalability, maintainability and security. The list is not limited to these requirements and varies in accordance with the decision policies of these organizations. Decisions are based on competitor offerings, costs, time and experience available with the organizations to implement the requirements.

RQ 5. How are nonfunctional requirements prioritized?

NFRs are not prioritized in software industries. Few NFRs are available for selection. Type of development specified whether the decision is made at once or in increments. Incremental decisions give the option to organizations to analyze competitor offerings to decide implementation set.

RQ 6. What is the extent to which the answers to the above questions depend on the maturity and size of software organization?

Maturity of organizations has an impact on the number of NFRs, ratio of NFR to FR, cost and time-share. It also varies with the complexity of the undertaken projects. With the increase in project complexity, the ratio decreases due to an enhanced number of FRs compared with nonfunctional ones. However, for matured organizations, the decrease is not steep because their vision allows them to focus on more NFRs than handled in less matured organizations. The ratio is higher for matured organization projects than less matured organization projects. The cost and time values are lower for matured organization than less matured ones. However, cost and time increase with an increase in project complexity.

RQ 7. How the present practices of the mobile development firms impact project success and failure rates?

The impact of missing NFR on project success increases with increase in project complexity and type of development (bespoke one-go to mass-market incremental). The abovementioned trends hold in both matured and less matured firms but are less in matured firms. The impact is less in matured firms than those with less matured firms but variation remains same with complexity. The quantitative details of failure rates were not given by software engineers because failure is a factor that each and every company tries to hide.

The empirical results indicate one more important finding relative to cost and time. The less number of NFRs results in less share in total cost and time (although varies among the organizations as discussed earlier). As researchers will focus more on NFRs due to result of the findings of this book, the cost and time percentage will increase considerably. Thus, NFRs focused development strategies require to consider the cost and time parameters as well.

In future, it is expected that the research community will find the empirical study reported in this book useful. This empirical study will motivate them to come up with innovative proposals for undertaking the suitable techniques for gathering and prioritization of NFRs to enhance the product success rates. The challenge will be the optimization of cost and time parameters as the NFRs catch greater attention of developers.

Chapter 5

Status of Nonfunctional Requirement in Mobile Application Development in Academic Projects

5.1 Academic Projects Survey/Case Study

The software projects implemented by the students are claimed to be industrial oriented. Hands-on experience on these projects helps the buddy engineers to learn new techniques, technologies and processes for undertaking quality software engineering. The ups and downs learned during academic projects help them to update their project database that could provide learning experience with industrial projects. The academic projects could find their applicability in industries and hence the quality of such software is important. Quality depends on the quality of software engineering practices. It is thus important to analyze that state of software development from nonfunctional requirements' (NFRs) point of view. The study is based on the objectives as established for industrial and literature studies performed in

Chapters 2 and 3 of this book. This work is an extension of the work given in previous chapters but in academic environment settings.

To answer the seven research questions as framed in Chapters 2 and 3 of this book, the 30 final year and pass out students belonging to both B. Tech and M. Tech academic programs were interviewed to get answers to the research questions. The responses obtained for each research question are given in the following.

RQ 1. What is the extent to which nonfunctional requirements get the software developers' attraction?

NFRs are the most ignored parts of academic projects. The reason is unrealistic deadline for submission (typically one semester), small team size (group) and less experience with similar projects. The effort is to complete the project in terms of its functional requirements (FRs) that will make enough justification that the project is working. Only very basic NFRs get the attraction of the developer and that is limited to security (username and password) and GUI. Again the students were of the opinion that it is not the nonfunctional ones that pay, but functional ones that get them good awards. Student projects are normally developed using one-go technique expect when they are to be extended as majors. In the latter case, extension is in the form of implementation of functional codes only.

RQ 2. What is the cost and time percentage of NFR in overall project cost and duration?

Cost of academic projects is hard to compute; however, the actual hours devoted by students in the development were collected from them. In the case of computer software projects, it is not possible to confirm the actual hours devoted since students can also work after official hours in their hostels or home. Student projects are medium complexity and low complexity with a total time percentage share of NFRs estimated to be 2% of the total project development time.

RQ 3. What is the implementation status of NFR to FR for different complexity projects?

The number of NFRs in academic projects is negligible as compared to functional projects. But, if still compared, the ratio comes out to be 0.12

Table 5.1   NFR to FR Ratios for Different Categories and Complexity Academic Projects

Sl. No.	Product Complexity	NFR to FR Ratio
1.	Medium	0.12
2.	Low	0.14

for medium-complexity projects and higher 0.14 for low-complexity projects. Typical ratios are given in Table 5.1.

Table 5.1 shows that there is no addition of NFRs with the increase in complexity of the academic projects. Complexity increase is attributable to increase in FRs.

RQ 4. What are the typical categories of NFRs implemented by mobile software developers?

Student academic projects are restricted to very basic NFRs, including security requirements like user name and password, database encryption and GUI requirements. Very few students had incorporated NFRs like multilanguage support, notifications and storage requirements. The reason reported by these students was that the application they developed would have made the app of no use if these three NFRs are not implemented. It means that NFRs for student projects depend on the nature of the functionality expected from the app.

RQ 5. How are nonfunctional requirements prioritized?

Students never prioritize the NFRs. The guidance from the project mentor about the NFRs is the only identification or selection criteria for NFRs.

RQ 6. What is the extent to which the answers to the above questions depend on the maturity and size of software organization?

The reputed universities or engineering colleges enable the students to implement projects on live research problems. Some innovative NFRs are considered, but the emphasis is to get automatization of the research problem solution. It means FRs are considered. Cost and time does not vary since the students are less experienced in implementing innovative NFRs and such requirements are less attractive to them. Good organization will consider innovative NFRs apart from basic ones, but prioritization never happens. Such projects are normally one-go projects.

RQ 7. How the present practices of the mobile development firms impact project success and failure rates?

The student projects are one-go-type projects or medium complexity. The feedback of the project mentor and evaluation committee is used as a means by the student to implement remaining requirements. Students were asked if they have to implement NFRs as a result of feedback. Student reported that for medium- or low-complexity projects, the mentors focus mostly on functionality. If functionality is satisfactory, students are asked to implement NFRs. However, the information was difficult to recall for the students. The outcome is that if functionality is completely implemented, then software is verified for NFRs. This means NFRs determine the success of student projects.

The findings of the academic projects survey are presented in Table 5.2.

5.2 Comparative Analysis

The findings of the industrial case studies, interviews and literature surveys are presented in Chapters 2 and 3. The findings are also compared with respect to each other. In this section, the academic project findings are compared with industrial survey results (Table 5.3). The outcomes from the comparative analysis of academic survey, industrial case study and industrial survey are leading to similar, and thus, academic findings are not individually compared with literature findings in this section. The similar outcomes of industrial case study, survey and academic survey are jointly compared in Table 4.10.

Further, the investigations of industrial findings are validated by increasing the sample size from 13 (with the experience of numerous projects) to 130. Employing such a large number of cases for such a big study and comparison with old findings was not feasible. So to check if the sample size provides any threat to findings, the findings (after it was accepted as a paper in one journal) were resubmitted to the remaining 117 software engineers. They were asked to rate the findings and inform us if additional information could be attached to the old findings. The new cases agreed to the findings, and thus the old findings were validated. The open-source statistical tool PSPP and other online available statistical tools were employed for analysis.

Table 5.2 Data Analysis of Academic Projects

Sl. No.	Research Question	Project Development and Complexity	Remarks
1.	RQ 1. What is the extent to which nonfunctional requirements get the software developers' attraction?	Medium and low	Little attention is paid. Students focus mainly on functional requirements.
2.	RQ 2. What is the cost and time percentage of NFR in overall project cost and duration?	Medium and low	Cost percentage is hard to computer. Time percentage share of NFR is 2% of the total time.
3.	RQ 3. What is the implementation status of NFR to FR for different complexity projects?	Medium and low	0.12 for medium- and 0.14 for low-complexity projects. With increase in complexity, only functional requirements increase rather than nonfunctional ones.
4.	RQ 4. What are the typical categories of NFRs implemented by mobile software developers?	Medium and low	Depends on the functionality of the app. NFR is restricted to basics ones like security and GUI.

(Continued)

Table 5.2 Data Analysis of Academic Projects (*Continued*)

Sl. No.	Research Question	Project Development and Complexity	Remarks
5.	RQ 5. How are nonfunctional requirements prioritized?	Medium and low	They are not subjected to any prioritization. Nonfunctional requirements as suggested by project mentor are implemented.
6.	RQ 6. What is the extent to which the answers to the above questions depend on the maturity and size of software organization?	Reputation, size of university/college	• Some innovative NFR considered. • Cost and time almost similar.
7.	RQ 7. How the present practices of the mobile development firms impact project success and failure rates?	One-go technique	• Nonfunctional requirements determine the success of student projects provided functional requirements are completely implemented.

Table 5.3 Comparative Analysis of Industrial and Academic Project Survey Results

Sl. No.	Research Question	Industrial Survey Analysis Results	Academic Project Survey Analysis Results	Comparative Results
1.	RQ 1. What is the extent to which nonfunctional requirements get the software developers' attraction?	Little attention is paid. Customers need to pay for nonfunctional ones or marginal cost used to pay partly for them. NFRs are also offered as free add-on features.	Little attention is paid. Students focus mainly on functional requirements.	NFRs get little attraction.
2.	RQ 2. What is the cost and time percentage of NFR in overall project cost and duration?	Cost percentage is 8% of the total cost and 19% of the total time (mass market). Cost percentage is in the range of 2–4% total cost and 3–6% of the total time (bespoke-incremental). Cost percentage is in the range of 2–3% total cost and 4–5% of the total time (bespoke one-go).	Cost percentage is hard to compute. Time percentage share of NFR is 2% of total time.	Although the number of NFRs is small in number yet has single-digit % age of cost and time. It varies with types of organization, development and complexity. Students and industrial projects are not comparable.

(Continued)

Table 5.3 Comparative Analysis of Industrial and Academic Project Survey Results (*Continued*)

Sl. No.	Research Question	Industrial Survey Analysis Results	Academic Project Survey Analysis Results	Comparative Results
3.	RQ 3. What is the implementation status of NFR to FR for different complexity projects?		0.12 for medium- and 0.14 for low-complexity projects. With increase in complexity only functional requirements increases rather than nonfunctional ones.	The ratio of the number of NFRs to FRs is smaller.
4.	RQ 4. What are the typical categories of NFRs implemented by mobile software developers?	No well-defined category. It depends on cost, time and functional requirements.	Depends on functionality of the app. NFR is restricted to the basic ones like security and GUI.	NFRs range from basic to slightly innovative ones. Cost, time and functional requirements determine NFRs.
5.	RQ 5. How are nonfunctional requirements prioritized?	They are not subjected to any prioritization. They are invented by the developer in accordance with what his experience says.	They are not subjected to any prioritization. Nonfunctional requirements as suggested by project mentor are implemented.	Prioritization practices are missing from practice.

| 6. | RQ 6. What is the extent to which the answers to the above questions depend on the maturity and size of software organization? | • NFRs from basic to innovative features depend on the maturity of the organization.
• Time, cost and ratio of NFR to FR depend on the maturity of the organization and type of development. | • Some innovative NFR considered.
• Cost and time almost similar. | Maturity or reputation incurs some innovative NFRs. Other parameters cannot be verified since industrial and students' projects are not comparable further as student projects do not have strict ways of computing costs and are based on one-go rather than incremental. Bespoke and mass markets are useless for such projects. |

(Continued)

Table 5.3 Comparative Analysis of Industrial and Academic Project Survey Results (*Continued*)

Sl. No.	Research Question	Industrial Survey Analysis Results	Academic Project Survey Analysis Results	Comparative Results
7.	RQ 7. How the present practices of the mobile development firms impact project success and failure rates?	• The impact of missing NFR on project success increases with increase in project complexity and type of development (bespoke one-go to mass market incremental). • The abovementioned trends hold in matured and less matured firms but are less in matured firms.	• Nonfunctional requirements determine the success of student projects provided functional requirements are completely implemented.	Students' projects and industrial projects exhibit similar trends, but student's projects are typically one-go small- or medium-complexity projects.

5.3 Conclusion

NFRs are ignored in academic settings. In typical student projects, the number of NFRs is almost negligible. The NFRs are costlier and take large time to get implemented. The contribution in total development cost and time is less due to less a number of NFRs selected for implementation. The number of NFRs in academic projects is negligible as compared to functional projects. More changes as suggested by faculty are functional in nature and hence nonfunctional are almost ignored. For academic projects, the NFRs are basic ones and hence students refrain from implementing complex NFRs. NFRs are not prioritized in academics. The reason is that students implemented very few NFRs and hence large alternatives are not available. The reputed universities or engineering colleges enable the students to implement projects on live research problems. Some innovative NFRs are considered, but the emphasis is to get automatization of the research problem solution. It means FRs are considered. Cost and time does not vary since the students are less experienced in implementing innovative NFRs and such requirements are less attractive to them. The student projects are one-go-type projects of medium complexity. The feedback of the project mentor and evaluation committee is used as a means by the student to implement the remaining requirements.

Chapter 6

Accuracy of Nonfunctional Requirement Prioritization Approaches for Different Complexity Projects: An Experimentation*

6.1 Introduction

Requirement prioritization is an activity to perform the selection of requirements, a task that is challenging due to the involvement of many stakeholders

* Reprinted from Perspectives in Science, Vol 8, Raj Kumar Chopra, Varun Gupta, Durg Singh Chauhan, Experimentation on accuracy of nonfunctional requirement prioritization approaches for different complexity projects, 79–82, 2016, with permission from Elsevier.

with potentially conflicting view points, multiple requirements to be handled and large effort to be invested in this activity. The wrong requirement selection not only results in wasteful effort and potentially increased effort of the next release, but also possesses the risk of project failures.

The software comprises functional and nonfunctional requirements that together determine the acceptability of it within the market. The users never demand the nonfunctional requirements but appreciate if they are implemented. The potential reason could be that nonfunctional requirements determine the success of functional aspects of the system and are usually unheard amongst its users. A user understands few of nonfunctional requirements after the software is put to use and other requirements as they interact with competitor products. For example, a mobile app with a good interface but with slow speed will not feel appealing to the users, and they may ask for fast applications.

The software could have many nonfunctional requirements that determine its success.

Resource constraints potentially being time and cost limitations put an end to the idea of implementation of all nonfunctional requirements, and hence, accuracy and effort-optimized prioritization is undertaken. However, the prioritization of nonfunctional requirements is challenging due to several reasons:

- Nonfunctional requirements are prioritized by developers and not by users. It is important that the selection of such requirements must be aligned to the selection of functional requirements.
- Nonfunctional requirements are always considered as the overhead as they do not provide any functional aspect to the system. Hence, investing huge effort in their selection and implementation is considered as only overhead effort for overall development. In other words, negligible resources are allocated for nonfunctional requirements.
- Nonfunctional requirements shall never be prioritized with respect to functional requirements, as competitive requirements. If this happens, nonfunctional requirements are guaranteed to get lower priority than functional requirements.
- Nonfunctional requirements can be prioritized individually, i.e. not in competition to functional requirements, but however, their selection needs to be balanced with the selected functional requirements.

However, there exist three approaches for the prioritization of nonfunctional requirements.

6.2 Nonfunctional Requirement Prioritization Approaches

The prioritization may employ existing requirement prioritization techniques using any of the three approaches:

- **Approach 1 (A1):** Prioritization of nonfunctional requirements together with functional requirements. This option is not a good option because nonfunctional requirements are guaranteed to lose in competition to functional aspects.
- **Approach 2 (A2):** Prioritization of nonfunctional requirements separately from functional requirements. This approach is the good approach as mostly nonfunctional requirements are prioritized by developers rather than users. But this is challenging because the selection of nonfunctional requirements depends on the selection of functional requirements with which they are associated.
- **Approach 3 (A3):** Hybrid of two approaches A1 and A2. In such a scheme, the nonfunctional requirements are given separate consideration but are selected in accordance with the prioritized functional requirements. There is no competition between nonfunctional and functional requirements for getting implemented in the current release. Thus, the selection is separate for both the two requirements, although selection depends on the functionality of the system.

6.3 Aim and Objectives

The aim of the chapter is to examine the effectiveness of the three prioritization approaches (A1, A2 and A3) for nonfunctional requirement prioritization for different complexity project versions. To fulfill the aim, this book is based on the two objectives, first, to examine the accuracy of the prioritization approaches by using the suitable prioritization technique on suitable software versions and, second, to analyze the impact of software complexity on the accuracy of prioritization approaches.

6.4 Experiment Details

To meet the objectives, experimentation is conducted using suitable software versions, employing a suitable requirement prioritization technique for each prioritization approach (A1, A2 and A3). The analytical hierarchical process

(AHP)-based cost-value prioritization technique (Karlsson and Ryan, 1997) is applied on three different complexity versions of same industrial software projects, i.e. versions belonging to low, medium and high complexity. This technique is employed because pairwise comparison–based prioritization technique had been found accurate by Karlsson (1996), Karlsson et al. (1998) and Perini et al. (2009). The time limitation for performing the prioritization was relaxed to control the scalability variable. The scalability variable would otherwise have influenced the relation between complexity and accuracy as pairwise comparison–based prioritization technique suffers from scalability issues as reported in Karlsson et al. (1998, 2004), Ahl (2005), Lehtola and Kauppinen (2006), Perini et al. (2009), Ribeiro et al. (2011), Voola and Babu (2013) and Achimugu et al. (2014). The experimentation units are summarized in Table 6.1.

The three versions of the selected project have 13 requirements (low complexity), 34 (medium) and 56 requirements (high complexity) to be subjected for prioritization. Low complexity project represents first increment, medium complexity represents the fourth increment and high complexity represents eight increment of mass market product. The increment details, i.e. the details of the number of requirements and categorization, are given in Table 6.2.

The projects are selected on the availability of project post-release statistics, i.e. project success measure (sale of software increments). The selected project versions/increments were having high success rates, and hence, the selected requirements for the release were considered as the benchmark representing high-quality prioritization. The selected project has a high number of nonfunctional requirements implemented in comparison to functional requirements.

Table 6.1   Experimentation Details

Sl. No.	Experimentation Units Category	Description of Units
1.	Requirement prioritization technique	Analytical hierarchical process (AHP) in the form of cost-value approach
2.	Projects number and complexity	One project with three versions, one of low complexity, one of medium and one of high
3.	Independent variable	Complexity
4.	Dependent variable	Accuracy
5.	Control variable	Scalability

Table 6.2 Software Version Details

Sl. No.	Complexity Project of Software	Requirements		Total Requirements (T)
		Functional	Nonfunctional	
1.	Low complexity	7	6	13
2.	Medium complexity	18	16	34
3.	High complexity	30	26	56

To measure the accuracy, the list of requirements as obtained after execution of cost-value approach on the three increments of the project individually were compared with the list of requirements implemented actually by the industry individually for different complexity projects. Large deviation between the current prioritization list and the one implemented by the industry earlier in actual for particular increment represents the less accuracy of the approach applied (A1, A2 or A3). A total of 20 experimentation units were involved in allocation of preferences for the requirements, which are experienced software engineers with long experiences in software development. Selection of requirements is a fresh process in the experimentation reported in this book. Thus, a number of requirements selected in each category and preferences need not to match those provided by industry.

6.5 Result Analysis

The execution of the prioritization technique employing three approaches individually on three complexity versions gives results that are analyzed at two levels namely,

- Comparative analysis of results for same complexity increment of three approaches gives an indication of accuracy of the approaches employed. The outcome is three results, one for each complexity project. Denote the results by R1, R2 and R3.
- Comparative analysis of the individual results (R1, R2 and R3) indicates the variation of accuracy with the complexity of the software increment.

Table 6.3   Experimentation Result Matrix

Sl. No.	Complexity	Approaches			Result
		A1	A2	A3	
1.	Low complexity	D1	D2	D3	R1
2.	Medium complexity	D4	D5	D6	R2
3.	High complexity	D7	D8	D9	R3

In other words, the execution of the experimentation will populate Table 6.3 with the results of execution. The results are given in Table 6.4.

Individual Ri indicates which approach is highly accurate for a given complexity project. Comparative analysis of Ri indicates the variation of accuracy of approaches with the project complexity. The table entries are in the form of a number (Di). Let N be the number of functional requirements and M be the nonfunctional requirements that match with the corresponding category requirement in both prioritization lists (current and those implemented by industry engineers) for a particular complexity project for a particular approach under consideration. The percentage of the number of requirements that matches is given by, $Di = (N + M)/T$, where T is the total number of requirements for a given complexity project (Table 6.2), for $i = 1 - 9$.

Table 6.4 data show very interesting results. The accuracy of approach A1 decreased with an increase in complexity. The major value of accuracy is contributed by the match between functional requirements, which means nonfunctional are ignored in competition. The accuracy of approach A2 is higher than A1 because of due consideration of nonfunctional requirements. The accuracy decreases with the increase in the complexity of the project, which means that as the number of requirements increases, the prioritization

Table 6.4   Experimentation Results

Sl. No.	Complexity	Approaches			Result (Better Approach)
		A1	A2	A3	
1.	Low complexity	0.44	0.73	0.92	A3
2.	Medium complexity	0.35	0.70	0.88	A3
3.	High complexity	0.25	0.62	0.91	A3

becomes complex to execute. But still the accuracy value is high enough for high-complexity projects. Approach A3 outperforms other approaches, which mean that consideration should be given to nonfunctional requirements by considering the functionality aspect. This is because nonfunctional requirements are associated with functional requirements. The accuracy remained higher for all complexity projects. The reason is that improvement is contributed due to improvement in the selection of nonfunctional requirements. The data show that the approach A3 outperforms other approaches, and with the increase in complexity, the accuracy of the approaches decreases. The decrease in accuracy is large in approach A1, lower in A2 and negligible in A3.

6.6 Conclusion

Nonfunctional requirements must be prioritized as separate entities like functional requirements, but their selection must be in accordance with the selected functionality of the software. For high-complexity software, the functionality-based selection of nonfunctional requirements enhances the success of the project. Selection of nonfunctional requirements without any reference to the functionality or competitive selection has low accuracy as the complexity of the software decreases; however, a competitive selection has low relative performance.

In future, it is expected that the requirement prioritization techniques for the selection of nonfunctional requirements based on system functionality will emerge in literature and real practice.

Chapter 7

Conclusion and Future Work

This chapter concludes that the nonfunctional requirements are equally important as functional requirements. Likewise a functional requirement that ensures utility of the software, nonfunctional requirements ensure the effective implementation of functionality. Such requirements impact the project success by impacting parameters like quality, cost, time and impact the business success of developing firms and client firms. The impact of missing nonfunctional requirements is hard for the business, and such business may be out from the market depending on severity, number and criticality of the nonfunctional requirements.

In future, it is expected that a suitable requirement prioritization techniques will be proposed that will strike a balance between functional and nonfunctional requirements. It is expected that the outcome of this book will motivate both the researchers and firms to invest resources to handle nonfunctional requirements. It is expected that in the near future, nonfunctional requirement–based prioritization techniques will be evaluated on both project and business success parameters to evaluate the success.

References

Achimugu P., Selamat A., Ibrahim R., Mahrin M., (2014). "A systematic literature review of software requirements prioritization research". *Information and Software Technology*, Vol. 56, pp. 568–585.

Ahl V., (2005). An experimental comparison of five prioritization methods – investigating ease of use, accuracy and scalability. Department of Systems and Software Engineering, School of Engineering, Sweden, Blekinge Institute of Technology, Master of Science in Software Engineering, 2005.

Avesani P., Bazzanella C., Perini A., Susi A., (2005). Facing scalability issues in requirements prioritization with machine learning techniques. *13th IEEE International Conference on Requirements Engineering (RE)*, France, pp. 297–306.

Bakalova Z., Daneva M., Herrmann A., Wieringa R., (2011). Agile requirements prioritization: what happens in practice and what is described in literature. *17th International Working Conference on Requirements Engineering: Foundation for Software Quality*.

Berander P., (2004). Using students as subjects in requirements prioritization. *International Symposium on Empirical Software Engineering (ISESE'04)*.

Capilla R., Babar M., Pastor O., (2012). "Quality requirements engineering for systems and software architecting: methods, approaches, and tools". *Requirements Engineering*, Vol. 17, pp. 255–258. DOI: 10.1007/s00766-011-0137-9.

Chung L., Sampaio do Prado Leite J.C., (2009). On non-functional requirements in software engineering. *Conceptual Modelling: Foundations and Applications*, pp. 363–379.

Dabbagh M., Lee S., (2015). "An approach for prioritizing NFRs according to their relationship with FRs". *Lecture Notes on Software Engineering*, Vol. 3, No. 1, pp. 1–5.

Dabbagh M., Lee S., (2014). "An approach for integrating the prioritization of functional and nonfunctional requirements". *The Scientific World Journal*, Vol. 2014, 13 pages

Daneva M., Kassab M., Ponisio M., Wieringa R., Ormandjieva O., (2007). Exploiting a Goal-Decomposition Technique. *10th International Workshop on Requirements Engineering, WER 2007*, 17–18 May 2007, Toronto, Canada, pp. 190–196.

Doerr J., Kerkow D., Koenig T., Olsson T., Suzuki T., (2005). Non-functional requirements in industry – three case studies adopting an experience-based NFR method. *13th IEEE International Conference on Requirements Engineering (RE'05).*

Fernandes T., Cota E., Moreira A., (2012). Performance evaluation of android applications: a case study. *2014 Brazilian Symposium on Computing Systems Engineering*, pp. 79–84.

Gruenbacher P., (2000). Collaborative requirements negotiation with EasyWinWin. *11th International Workshop on Database and Expert Systems Applications.*

Gupta V., Srivastav M., (2011). "Web based tool supported requirement prioritization: based on multiple stakeholder preferences". International Journal on Computer Engineering and Information Technology (IJCEIT), Vol. 25, No. 1, pp 12–19.

Gupta V., Chauhan D., Dutta K., (2011b). Hybrid regression testing technique: a multi layered approach. *IEEE Annual Conference "INDICON"*, Hyderabad, IEEE, DOI: 10.1109/INDCON.2011.6139363.

Gupta V., Chauhan D., Dutta K., (2012a). "Hybrid decision aspect prioritization technique for globally distributed developments". Procedia Engineering, Vol. 38, pp. 3614–3627. DOI: http://dx.doi.org/10.1016/j.proeng.2012.06.418.

Gupta V., Chauhan D., Dutta K., (2012b). "Impact analysis of requirement prioritization on regression testing". AWER Procedia Information Technology & Computer Science, Vol. 2, pp. 379–383.

Gupta V., Chauhan D.S., Dutta K., (2012c). "Regression testing based requirement prioritization of mobile applications". International Journal of Systems and Service-Oriented Engineering (IJSSOE), Vol. 3, No. 4, pp. 20–39.

Gupta V., Chauhan D., Dutta K., (2013a). Incremental Development & Revolutions of E-Learning Software Systems in Education Sector: A Case Study Approach. Human-Centric Computing and Information Sciences (HCIS), Vol. 3, No. 8.

Gupta V., Chauhan D., Dutta K., (2013b). "Requirement reprioritization: a multilayered dynamic approach". International Journal of Software Engineering and Its Applications, 7(5), 55–64.

Gupta V., Chauhan D.S., Dutta K., (2013c). "Regression testing based requirement prioritization of desktop applications". International Journal of Software Engineering and Its Applications, Vol. 7, No. 6, pp. 9–18.

Gupta V., Chauhan D., Dutta K., (2015a). "Hybrid regression testing based on path pruning". International Journal of Systems and Service-Oriented Engineering (IJSSOE), Vol. 1, No. 5, pp. 35–55.

Gupta V., Chauhan D., Dutta K., (2015b). "Requirement prioritization of Web 2.0 application based on effects on regression testing: an hybrid approach". International Journal of Systems and Service-Oriented Engineering (IJSSOE), Vol. 5, No. 3, pp. 18–37.

Gupta V., Chauhan D., Dutta K., (2015c). "Exploring reprioritization through systematic literature surveys and case studies". SpringerPlus, Vol. 4, p. 539. DOI: 10.1186/s40064-015-1320-0.

Gupta V., Chauhan D., Dutta K., (2016). "Historical prioritization & reprioritization using hierarchical historical R-tree (HHR-tree)". International Journal of Computer Applications in Technology (IJCAT). ~, 54(4), pp. 257–265

Happach S., (11th December, 2012). *mCommerce in India: The Opportunity.* UK: The Huffington Post. Retrieved on 22nd January, 2013 from http://www.huffington-post.co.uk/shane-happach/mcommerce-in-india-the-op_b_2115871.html.

Huang J., Denne M., (2005). Financially informed requirements prioritization. *27th International Conference on Software Engineering (ICSE 2005)*.

Hindle A., (2015). "Green mining: a methodology of relating software change and configuration to power consumption". Empirical Software Engineering, Vol. 20, pp. 374–409. DOI: 10.1007/s10664-013-9276-6.

Jim A., Randy S., David C., (2007). Value-oriented requirements prioritization. IEEE Software, 24(1), 32–37.

Karlsson J., (1996). Software requirements prioritizing. *Second International Conference on Requirement Engineering*, pp. 110–116.

Karlsson J., Ryan K., (1997). "A cost-value approach for prioritizing requirements". IEEE Software, 4(5), pp. 67–74.

Karlsson J., Wohlin C., Regnell B., (1998). "An evaluation of methods for prioritizing software requirements". Journal of Information and Software Technology, Vol. 39, No. 14–15, pp. 939–947.

Karlsson L., Berander P., Regnell B., Wohlin C., (2004). Requirements prioritisation: an experiment on exhaustive pair-wise comparisons versus planning game partitioning. *Proceedings of the 8th International Conference on Empirical Assessment in Software Engineering (EASE 2004)*, Edinburgh, Scotland.

Kitchenham B., Charters, S. (2007). "Guidelines for performing systematic literature reviews in software engineering", version 2.3. EBSE Technical Report EBSE-2007-01, Keele University and University of Durham.

Koziolek A., (2012). Architecture-driven quality requirements prioritization. *2012 IEEE First International Workshop on the Twin Peaks of Requirements and Architecture (Twin Peaks)*.

Kukreja N., Payyavula S., Boehm B., Padmanabhuni S., (2012). Selecting an appropriate framework for value-based requirements prioritization a case study. *2012 20th IEEE International Requirements Engineering Conference (RE)*.

Laplante P., (2009). Requirements Engineering for Software and Systems, 1st edn. CRC Press, Redmond, WA.

Lehtola L., Kauppinen M., Kujala S., (2004). Requirements prioritization challenges in practice. Product Focused Software Process Improvement, pp. 497–508.

Lehtola L., Kauppinen M., (2006). "Suitability of requirements prioritization methods for market-driven software product development". Software Process Improvement and Practice, Vol. 11, p. 7–19. DOI: 10.1002/spip.249.

Mylopoulos J., Chung L., Nixon B., (1992). "Representing and using nonfunctional requirements: a process-oriented approach". IEEE Transactions on Software Engineering, Vol. 18. No. 6, pp. 483–497.

Norbert Seyff N., Todoran I., Caluser K., Singer L., Glinz M., (2015). "Using popular social network sites to support requirements elicitation, prioritization and negotiation". Journal of Internet Service and Applications". DOI: 10.1186/s13174-015-0021-9, 6(7), pp. 1–16.

Orsini G., Bade D., Lamersdorf W., (2015). "Context-aware computation offloading for mobile cloud computing: requirements analysis, survey and design guideline". Procedia Computer Science, Vol. 56, pp. 10–17.

Perini A., Ricca F., Susi A., (2009). "Tool supported requirement prioritization: comparing the AHP and CBRank methods". Information and Software Technology, Vol. 51, pp. 1021–1032.

Perini A., Susi A., Ricca F., Bazzanella C., (2007). An empirical study to compare the accuracy of AHP and CBRanking techniques for requirements prioritization. *Fifth International Workshop on Comparative Evaluation in Requirements Engineering*, pp. 23–35.

Racheva Z., Daneva M., Buglione L., (2008). Supporting the dynamic reprioritization of requirements in agile development of software products. *Second International Workshop on Software Product Management*.

Racheva Z., Daneva M., Herrmann A., Wieringa R., 2010a. A conceptual model and process for client-driven agile requirements prioritization. *4th International Conference on Research challenges in Information Science (RCIS)*.

Racheva Z., Daneva M., Herrmann A., 2010b. A conceptual model of client-driven agile requirements prioritization: results of a case study. *ACM-IEEE International Symposium on Empirical Software Engineering and Measurement*.

Ribeiro R., Moreira A., Broek P., Pimentel A., (2011). "Hybrid assessment method for software engineering decisions". Decision Support Systems, Vol. 51, pp. 208–219.

Singh S.K., (27th August, 2012). *Future of mCommerce Services In India*. India: InsightVAS. Retrieved on 22nd January, 2013 from http://insightvas.com/future-of-mcommerce-services-in-india/.

Selvarani D., Ravi T., (2012) "A survey on data and transaction management in mobile databases". International Journal of Database Management Systems (IJDMS), Vol. 4, No. 5, pp. 1–20.

Svensson R., Gorschek T., Regnell B., Torkar R., Shahrokni A., Feldt R., Aurum A., (2011). Prioritization of quality requirements: state of practice in eleven companies. *2011 IEEE 19th International Requirements Engineering Conference*.

Srikanth H., Williams L., Osborne J., (2005). System test case prioritization of new and regression test cases. *International Symposium on Empirical Software Engineering*.

Srikanth H., Williams L., (2005). On economic benefits of system level test case prioritization. *International Conference on Software Engineering*, St. Loius, MO.

Srivastav P., Kumar K., Raghurama G., (2008). "Test case prioritization based on requirements and risk factors". ACM SIGSOFT Software Engineering Notes, Vol. 33, No. 4, pp. 1–5.

Türker C., Zini G., (2003). "A survey of academic and commercial approaches to transaction support in mobile computing environments". Technical Report, ETH Zurich.

Voola P., Babu A., (2013). "Comparison of requirements prioritization techniques employing different scales of measurement". ACM SIGSOFT Software Engineering Notes, Vol. 38, No. 4.

Wiegers K., (1999a). Software Requirements. Microsoft Press, Redmond, Washington.

Wiegers K., (1999b). "First things first: prioritizing requirements". Software Development, Vol. 7, No. 9, pp.48–53.

Wordpayglobalonlineshopperfromhttp://www.worldpay.com/corporate/index.php?page= reports&sub=global-online-shopper&c=WW.

Index

Printed in the United States
by Baker & Taylor Publisher Services